D0460568

ORIENTEERING

OUTDOOR PURSUITS SERIES

Tom Renfrew

University of Strathclyde

Human Kinetics

Library of Congress Cataloging-in-Publication Data

Renfrew, Tom.
   Orienteering / Tom Renfrew.
     p.   cm. -- (Outdoor pursuits series)
   Includes index.
   ISBN 0-87322-885-5
   1. Orienteering.   I. Title. II. Series.
  GV200.4.R46   1997
  796.5' 1--dc20   96-10885
                                         CIP

ISBN: 0-87322-885-5

Copyright © 1997 by Human Kinetics Publishers, Inc.

Maps courtesy of the Scottish Orienteering Association.

Series Editor and Developmental Editor: Holly Gilly; **Assistant Editors:** Chad Johnson and Henry Woolsey; **Editorial Assistant:** Amy Carnes; **Copyeditor:** John Wentworth; **Proofreader:** Erin Cler; **Indexer:** Theresa Schaefer; **Typesetter:** Ruby Zimmerman; **Layout Artist:** Stuart Cartwright; **Text Designer:** Keith Blomberg; **Photo Editor:** Boyd LaFoon; **Cover Designer:** Jack Davis; **Photographer (cover):** Jonathan Taylor; **Illustrators:** Thomas • Bradley Illustration & Design and Jennifer Delmotte

Human Kinetics books are available at special discounts for bulk purchase. Special editions or book excerpts can also be created to specification. For details, contact the Special Sales Manager at Human Kinetics.

Printed in Hong Kong   10 9 8 7 6 5 4 3 2 1

Human Kinetics
Web site: http://www.humankinetics.com/

United States: Human Kinetics
P.O. Box 5076, Champaign, IL 61825-5076
1-800-747-4457
e-mail: humank@hkusa.com

Canada: Human Kinetics, Box 24040, Windsor, ON N8Y 4Y9
1-800-465-7301 (in Canada only)
e-mail: humank@hkcanada.com

Europe: Human Kinetics, P.O. Box IW14, Leeds LS16 6TR, United Kingdom
(44) 1132 781708
e-mail: humank@hkeurope.com

Australia: Human Kinetics, 57A Price Avenue, Lower Mitcham, South Australia 5062
(08) 277 1555
e-mail: humank@hkaustralia.com

New Zealand: Human Kinetics, P.O. Box 105-231, Auckland 1
(09) 523 3462
e-mail: humank@hknewz.com

CONTENTS

Chapter 5 The Best Places to Orienteer 73

Chapter 6 Pursuing Orienteering Further 97

Appendix For More Information 111

Orienteering Lingo 121

Index 125

About the Author 129

1

GOING ORIENTEERING

People have always felt the need

to explore, to push back the frontier. Early civilizations ventured into new lands when food became scarce, when the climate changed, or when they felt threatened. Explorers, such as Marco Polo, Christopher Columbus, James Cook, Daniel Boone, and John Wesley Powell, are part of our folklore, and their discoveries helped shape nation-states. By the 20th century the world was almost completely mapped, yet explorers continued to seek further challenges, including lunar and space expeditions.

Most of us are naturally curious and retain a strong desire to discover the wonders of new places. Adventurers among us are not content to do this discovering by car —they take to the hills, deserts, and forests with maps and compasses to blaze new trails (and to rediscover old ones). They love the thrill and challenge of planning and executing routes that lead to places they've never been before.

Orienteering, a relatively new and fast-growing sport, appeals to the adventurer's need to explore. With unfamiliar terrain as the playing field, orienteering requires speed, agility, endurance, and the ability to read and interpret complex maps on the run. Called the "thought sport" or "cunning running," the sport is a great activity for people who want to get off the beaten path (or track) and think on their feet. Hundreds of thousands of people the world over already are engaged in orienteering competitively.

Why Orienteering Is for You

If you're looking for a sport that makes demands on both your mind and body, orienteering is perfect for you. Many newcomers enjoy running or "keeping fit" activities but find it dull running laps or alongside a highway. If you are attracted to the forest or remote countryside, you will enjoy the challenge of orienteering. If you become an orienteer, you'll also enjoy the company of others who are attracted to an outdoor lifestyle and the thrilling satisfaction of navigating through wild, unfamiliar terrain.

It doesn't matter how old you are or how fit you are. Orienteering is a versatile sport that takes many forms, including cross-country orienteering, score orienteering, ski orienteering, or mountain bike orienteering. The sport can be pursued in several settings, each demanding its own level of technical and physical skill.

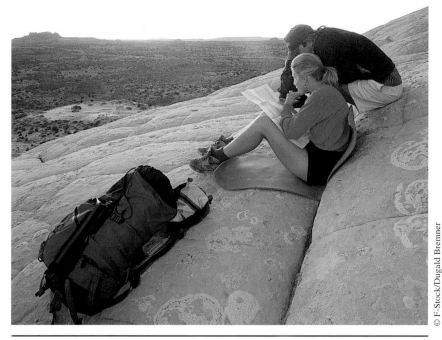

© F-Stock/Dugald Bremner

Orienteering skills can be used in many settings.

IN THE BEGINNING

Orienteering has its origins in Sweden, a country with a wealth of natural forests. At the start of this century, Ernst Killander, a Swedish Youth and Scout leader, noting a decline in track and field athletics, decided to try to involve young people more in the natural environment. He began by setting simple problems of route finding that challenged youths both mentally and physically. Encouraged by the response he received, he extended his ideas and, by 1922, enough youths were participating for district tournaments to be held. In years to come, the clarity of maps used by competitors improved, and track runners and skiers who had won the early races needed to develop map skills to continue their success.

The sport developed without expensive equipment or clothing, most competitors ran in old clothes and training shoes. In 1938, the Swedish Orienteering Federation (SOFT) was founded, which allowed orienteering clubs to unite. The federation also helped push the sport into other European countries. By 1961, orienteering had spread so far that the International Orienteering Federation (IOF) was formed.

At present, the IOF has 45 member federations from five continents. All over the world, enthusiastic and experienced orienteers act as missionaries, helping "new" countries develop mapping, competition, and coaching.

Orienteering is a fast-growing worldwide sport. Its growth cannot be attributed to a high media profile because it is a participant sport, not a spectator sport. Its governing bodies are not cash wealthy, so little money trickles down to the hundreds of clubs worldwide; most clubs spend any income on mapping new terrain. Yet the sport continues to grow, new clubs are springing into existence, new forests are being mapped, and new countries are forming associations that will eventually affiliate to the International Orienteering Federation.

A main attraction of orienteering is its simple structure—it is run totally by its participants. Orienteers make their own maps, plan their own courses, and organize their own events. Competitions are set up according to age, experience, and level of technical competence. The sport is expanding all the time, welcoming newcomers and going to great lengths to encourage and help any new participant.

In many European countries, particularly in Scandinavia, orienteering is a family activity in which parents and children compete, either individually on courses especially designed to match their age and experience levels, or

Orienteering is the ideal activity for families to do together.

as a family group. In the United States and other countries that have more recently adopted the sport, orienteering is less family oriented and more for adventure-sport athletes and fitness enthusiasts.

Today, hundreds of thousands of people orienteer worldwide, and new countries join the International Orienteering Federation each year. Orienteering has gained a reputation as an inexpensive sport that graciously welcomes new participants. It offers an alternative healthy recreational opportunity that is hard to resist.

Orienteering is thriving today mainly because it has many benefits other sports can't claim:

- An inexpensive and safe access to adventure activity
- A nonelitist approach and a reputation for welcoming and helping newcomers
- A club structure that allows for meeting people with similar interests and backgrounds
- A cleansing, back-to-nature experience in peaceful outdoor settings
- A pursuit that challenges both the body and mind

- An activity that can be done either individually or in teams and either competitively or noncompetitively

Wherever you live, you can easily find a place to orienteer, choosing either to share the experience with friends and family or to savor it for yourself. Enthusiasts may travel all over the world to pursue their sport, but their early experiences are usually local.

Finding Competition

A major appeal of orienteering is that it can accommodate a wide range of ages and abilities. Its simple concept and format allows participation in a variety of settings. Orienteering clubs have a keen eye for areas that offer good ground for challenging their map skills and fitness levels. Excellent five-color maps exist for thousands of forests, and many of these quality areas hold major championships or international competitions. In addition, many suburban parks and small areas of woodland on the edge of towns or cities have been mapped and are used for local competitions and training. The development of the sport worldwide follows a common pattern: Groups of orienteers form a local club and then affiliate to their National Orienteering Federation.

Clubs organize small meets on conveniently located terrain. These meets are held not only for members, but to attract newcomers. Such events typically offer a limited selection of courses, but they normally include a course for beginners, including first-timers. Instruction is usually coordinated by meet organizers who designate one or more persons to teach newcomers the basic techniques required for a beginner's course.

As clubs grow, they put on major, but still local, meets with a greater range of courses. Often, competitors from neighboring clubs will travel to these meets. The orienteering season also includes a number of nationally sanctioned meets offering a full range of courses. Such meets often require competitors to preregister. Meets are advertised in the local press and also in the federation's magazine.

Smaller local meets often have color-coded courses rather than age-group courses. Color coding of orienteering courses has been introduced worldwide to ensure standardization. The colors classify the courses according to length and technical difficulty. Lighter colors indicate shorter, technically easier courses for beginners or children and darker colors indicate longer, more challenging courses. Small differences in color coding exist from country to country, but the well established British system is the basis for most color-coded courses. The events standards chart on page 27 describes what the colors indicate.

Nationally sanctioned meets are entered according to your age on December 31 of the current year. A range of courses planned by national guidelines is available for both men and women. Course distances vary according to the nature of the terrain, and course planners use technical and physical guidelines when planning age-group courses. The chart on page 8 describes the characteristics of various levels of difficulty course planners consider. Call the event's organizer for information about the exact location of the meets.

In 1993 the USOF held the orienteering world championships, and the federation linked this prestigious event to a public orienteering festival. The courses were mapped in Harriman State Park in New York's Hudson Valley and demonstrated that United States orienteering has a technical ability, terrain, and beauty that is hard to match.

A Sport for All Ages

Orienteering caters to every age group. The 1994 World Veterans' Orienteering Championships held in Scotland included competitors over 90

© CompassSport/James Bearce

Whether a beginner or an elite athlete, orienteering is a sport anyone can enjoy.

years of age. At the other end of the scale, children less than school age can participate in a string course (a course marked with a continuous line of string) while the rest of the family compete in color-coded courses that suit their age and ability.

Orienteering's progressive activities encourage families to take up this sport, where everyone participates rather than watches. As youngsters take part and progress in orienteering, they learn to read maps and to care for the outdoors. These lessons have long been recognized as worthwhile by educators, and orienteering is on the curriculum of many schools and colleges. European schools have their own school maps and use orienteering to cover several aspects of the curriculum (i.e., mathematics, language, and science) simultaneously, rather than through isolated individual lessons. Orienteering is a great tool for doing this, especially if the students are participating actively.

Orienteering for Children

Orienteering appeals to children of all ages and aptitudes. Whether as a sport, recreational activity, or school exercise, orienteering offers exploration, problem solving, challenge, and exciting running. Once children have

Courtesy of Orienteering World

Running a string course is a good way for young children to become acquainted with orienteering skills.

TECHNICAL AND PHYSICAL CHARACTERISTICS OF DIFFICULTY LEVELS

Distances will vary according to the roughness of the terrain.

Level 1 (Easy)

Technical

- Controls on line features
- Controls close together
- No route choice
- Routes follow line features

-

Physical

- Minimum amount of climbing
- Avoid undergrowth and green areas
- Use best available terrain

Level 3 (Medium)

Technical

- Controls on easier point features
- Controls near obvious attack points
- Catching line features behind controls
- Some route choice
- Direct routes quickest but longer alternatives available
- Encourage simple use of contour detail

Physical

- Some climbing, no extended climbs
- Only short distances through green areas

Level 5 (Hard)

Technical

- Controls on any features but not hidden
- Controls far from collecting features
- Errors at controls expensive
- Legs demanding a range of techniques
- Legs across slopes

Physical

- Climbing as necessary for good planning
- Green areas acceptable but minimize

grasped the basic techniques of the sport, they can progress through the color-coded system of their age class and run competitively against others.

Children may do their first orienteering at school or summer camp, where the emphasis is likely on map reading. Initially the maps are probably of the school or campgrounds, or even of a smaller area such as the teacher's desk, the classroom, or the gymnasium. Eventually a real orienteering experience is offered in the local park or woodland. Joining the local orienteering club is a natural progression for children who show an interest or aptitude for the sport.

© CompassSport/George Crawford Smith

Even the youngest can find something to enjoy in orienteering!

Progressive orienteering clubs offer a teaching/training program to their juniors. The program shows how the demands of orienteering relate to the child's development. The emphasis is on enjoyment and success through repetitive learning experiences that progress naturally from each stage to the next. One example of good practice is the "Swedish Step System," a tried and tested system recommended by the International Orienteering Federation. This system is popular with teachers and coaches, as it classifies orienteering techniques progressively as a series of steps which children or beginners move up as they make progress. A chart showing the skills mastered with each step can be found on the next page. The system stresses the need to master techniques at step 1 before moving up to the techniques at step 2 and ensures that beginners do not attempt techniques that are beyond their skill level. If your child joins an orienteering club ask club officials, or the club coach, if they use the step-by-step approach.

For children doing string and white courses, the United States Orienteering Federation (USOF) sponsors a 4-level program called the "Little Troll" program. At each level the child does the appropriate course and, when

SWEDISH STEP SYSTEM

Level	Contents
Step 6	Difficult control points
	Pacing
	Longer legs and longer distance to catching features and attack point
Step 5	Using the correct technique with changes in difficulty
	Reading contours at competition speed
	Check-point routes
Step 4	M Reading contours in detail
	L Orienteering using large knolls and significant re-entrants
	K Understanding contours
Step 3	I Fine orienteering on short legs
	H Rough orienteering on longer legs against catching features
	G Making simple route choices
Step 2	F Orienteering on short legs against catching features
	E Shortcuts
	D Reading objects by paths, taking controls just off a path
Step 1	C Orienteering from path to path
	B Orienteering along a single path
	A Map colors, most commonly used symbols, and orienting the map using terrain
Ground level	Understanding the map, orienting the map, getting used to being in the woods

finished, is given a sticker to place on a Little Troll card. When the required number of stickers has been collected, the card can be sent to the USOF headquarters, which sends the child a badge and a new card.

Many other countries throughout the orienteering world use similar incentive schemes to give children the opportunity to take part in courses at the appropriate level. Above all, these courses are designed to motivate youngsters to continue in the sport.

A Family Adventure

Many adults, myself included, become involved in orienteering because their children are active in the sport. Whereas in many sports a parent's role is limited to spectating or officiating, in orienteering the whole family can actively participate. On meet days, lunch is prepared, clothing and equipment packed, and the family sets out together to seek common experiences.

Once at the meet, start times can be staggered to allow adults and children to compete and the youngest to enjoy a string course. Following competition, maps can be exchanged and routes discussed. If major errors have occurred, parent and child can revisit control sites or parts of the course to determine what went wrong. It's not unusual to see a parent shadowing (running behind) a child over a leg of the course—not as a competitor, but to experience the run with the child.

After all family members have finished their activities and checked their results on the leaderboard, it's time to chat with friends and fellow competitors, who are always ready to discuss their run. Participants have the chance to praise (or sympathize with) each other's performances with knowledge and understanding of the challenges of the course.

After lunch, family members—and sometimes other club members—visit a local area of historic or other interest. No matter how the rest of the day is spent, members of the family remain linked by their common experience of orienteering.

Getting Started

Although successful orienteering demands mastering certain basic techniques, most of these are easy to learn and develop. In the beginning, try relatively easy terrain, such as city parks or open spaces, where permanent courses may be laid out by the orienteering clubs. Next, you may want to try competing in local club events. Most clubs provide coaching and training for their members. While you are learning and practicing the techniques of the sport, you'll also be improving your physical fitness. Soon—usually within a year, if you practice regularly—you'll be ready for competitions in more demanding forests.

Orienteering meets are held on most weekends throughout the year in a well-organized competitive structure. They are also run on midweek evenings when daylight allows. The best way to get started is to contact your nearest club or association (see appendix for addresses) and attend a local meet.

A DAY IN THE FOREST

The competitive season is nearing its end. Elation after a good run, despondency over a missed control, or, even worse, frustration at missing an event because of an injury are almost forgotten. My ranking number has dropped this year. Is it from lack of fitness or poor technique? Whatever the cause, I am still keen to improve next year when I move up into another age group.

Anyway, this season ends with perhaps the most enjoyable experience of the year—a 6-day holiday event in Scotland, including orienteering every day with family, friends, and club members in a magnificent setting.

The first day dawns bright. The journey from our campsite is short but spectacularly beautiful. I am nervous as I line up at the start, where I can hear voices from Sweden, France, Australia, and many other parts of the world. I try to concentrate on the course and visualize that first important control.

The buzzer sounds on the start line, and I am off, running toward the box that contains my map. I am tempted to keep running as I pick it up, but my mind is well focused. Experience ensures that I stop, orient the map, examine the challenge of the first leg, and work out a suitable route.

I calculate the leg to be about 650 meters long and estimate that the best route lies almost in a straight line. Using my compass, I set off for the prominent hill (A), more than halfway to the control. I run along the edge of the marsh, using it as a handrail, as I would a path. The sound of a deer running breaks my concentration. Suddenly, the deer is only a short distance from me, standing motionless in the sunlight, watching me curiously. I have come too close, so it turns and runs uphill into the protection of the forest.

I force myself to concentrate and take a deep breath, marveling at the purity of the air. My senses are unusually keen. Above the sound of the

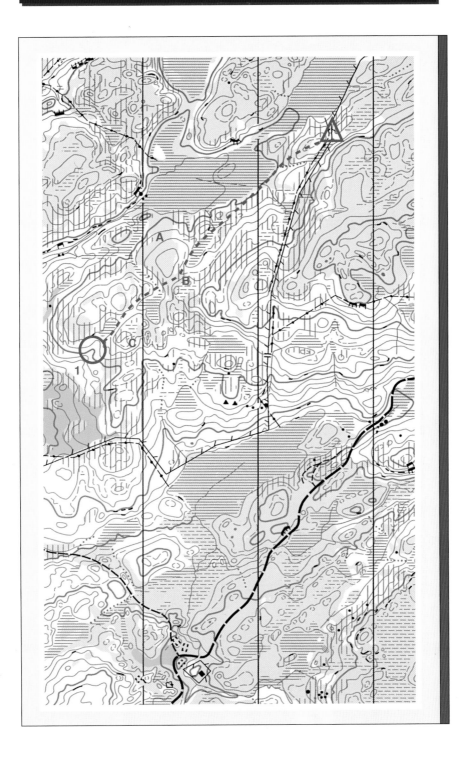

birds, I can hear my shoes squelching in the damp undergrowth. I pass two small knolls just before the hill and decide to skirt the hill to the south. I cross a narrow marsh (B) and calculate that I am about 150 meters from the control. I am now in an undulating, more heavily wooded area, and I slow down as I move slightly uphill. Where is the linear marsh near to my control that I'm using to attack the control site? I see another competitor running confidently at right angles to my direction of travel. I stop, momentarily debating whether to follow her, wondering if she is going for my control. Common sense and experience prevail, and I decide to ignore her. Instead, I examine my map carefully and relate it to the terrain around me—but I must keep moving.

I see a small knoll on my left (C). The marsh should be just a little further on my right. I veer to the right, slightly downhill, and, to my relief, run straight into the linear marsh that I am using to attack the control, a prominent re-entrant.

I feel deeply satisfied at successfully completing the first leg—even more so as I look up from punching my card to see a clear, sparkling lake, dotted with islands. I'm tempted to stop and appreciate the view, but I regain my concentration and set off for the next control.

This is the start of a day of adventure in the forest: a rare mix of fresh air, pleasant scenery, and the joy that comes from combined mental and physical activity.

2

ORIENTEERING EQUIPMENT

No matter what outdoor pursuit you decide to take up, you'll probably need to buy appropriate clothes and equipment. Depending on the activity you choose, you may also need to find a suitable way of storing your equipment. An industry has developed around the manufacture of canoes, skis, mountain bikes, and many other expensive items of equipment. Whatever the pursuit, participants need some form of clothing, often protective, and many clothing items are stylishly designed and attractive. This has resulted in essential clothing sometimes being considered fashionable and bought by the general public as leisure wear. Fashions change, and with the change comes the temptation to buy the latest ski suit, wet suit, or helmet in order to conform or feel good.

The arrival of large manufacturing companies into the outdoor pursuit market has brought benefits in terms of high quality goods, sponsorship for the sport, and much needed media coverage. On the downside, however, the need for increasing expenditure to participate sometimes restricts access to those who can afford it.

With the way things are, you'll be happy to hear that orienteering is a relatively inexpensive sport to take up, as elaborate equipment and expensive protective clothing are not required.

Clothing and Footwear

You want good value for your money. This means clothes and shoes that fit you correctly, suit your special needs, wash well, and generally last. For now, don't go out and buy all the clothing and footwear you see experienced orienteers wearing—wait at least until you have tried several meets or training days. To begin, wear comfortable, fairly old sports clothing such as a tracksuit top and pants and athletic training shoes. Don't worry, you won't feel at all out of place, as the majority of experienced orienteers you see in stylish club orienteering suits probably started the same way. After participating for a month or so over different terrain in different climatic conditions, you'll be better able to determine your exact needs for clothing and other gear.

Orienteers have generally resisted overpriced fashion clothing. Most participants wear an inexpensive light nylon suit for competition. The lightweight nylon provides some protection from prickly undergrowth without restricting movement. Most clubs have their own multicolored designs with matching tracksuits or sweatshirts. Shorts are less suitable, as they give no protection to the legs.

© CompassSport/Hazelle Jackson

You don't have to buy special clothing for orienteering. Everyday exercise clothes are perfect.

In most places where it is popular, orienteering does not have a distinct season, but meet organizers usually avoid months when the weather may be extreme because very cold or hot weather can take the pleasure out of competing and could be dangerous. With this in mind, you can safely show up for your first meet wearing light tracksuit pants and a T-shirt. In cold or wet weather, you may need extra layers and a light waterproof jacket, particularly if the meet moves out of the protection of the forest onto moorland or other open land. Remember that as a beginner you'll need to stop frequently to read your map, which means you may cool down rapidly in cold weather. Keep this in mind when deciding how much clothing to wear.

Consider buying a pair of protective leg gaiters. These light nylon accessories zip neatly around your shins over the top of your pants and provide worthwhile extra protection in rough terrain.

© CompassSport/Hazelle Jackson

Gaiters help keep your shins protected in rough terrain.

Don't take on any part of a course without comfortable footwear. Orienteers normally wear specially designed studded shoes that resemble soccer boots. Forests tend to retain water, so expect your feet to get wet and plan ahead.

Orienteering shoes are tough and made to protect your feet from branches, undergrowth, and rocky ground. Expect to pay about $70 for a good pair. If you clean and dry them after each meet, they should last for 4 or 5 years. Shoes that provide ankle support are also growing in popularity.

In general, make sure that the shoes you buy fit well, have studded soles to help them grip in wet or muddy terrain, and have a strong upper that will resist tears and scratches from prickly undergrowth. A couple of hours spent choosing strong and comfortable orienteering shoes is time well spent.

SAFETY TIP Always use shoelaces long enough to tie into a double bow. Tape this bow to ensure that it does not untie during the competition. You can't run with your shoes untied, and you don't want to waste time retying laces when you're competing.

Compasses

The most expensive piece of equipment you'll need is a compass, an invaluable instrument for precise navigation. Skillfully used, your compass will enable you to keep the map oriented, select more direct routes, and follow them faster while referring to the map.

There are many good compasses on the market. One of the most important qualities to look for is a magnetic needle that settles quickly as you move the compass around. There are two types of compasses most common for orienteering: the protractor compass and the thumb compass. The clip compass is also a good choice for the beginning orienteer.

Expect to pay from $15 to $70 for a protractor compass and from $40 to $80 for a thumb compass. The map or clip compass can be purchased for $15 or less. Most manufacturers design compasses with similar features including distance-measuring scales, small built-in magnifiers, and a wrist cord. The most expensive compasses are designed to allow the magnetic needle to settle quickly after movement. Protractor compasses are generally available from outdoor retailers, but the more specialized thumb and clip compasses can only be obtained from the traders who attend orienteering meets.

If you take care of your compass—that is, avoid dropping it or shaking it too much—it should last several years. Likely, you'll want to buy a new one every four or five seasons, or sooner if it shows any signs of wear. The most common signs of wear include the needle taking time to settle and large bubbles appearing in the liquid-dampened housing. You may ignore small bubbles that don't affect the needle, as they often disappear with temperature or altitude changes.

AT A GLANCE—COMPASSES

Type	Strengths	Weaknesses	Price
Protractor	Multipurpose use outside of orienteering. Easier to use when slowly following a bearing.	Encourages beginners to look at compass needle at the expense of map reading.	$15-$70
Thumb	Encourages use of compass and map as one unit. Leaves one hand free.	Difficult to use when slowly following a bearing. Restricted to use for orienteering.	$40-$80
Clip	Encourages use of compass and map as one unit. Simplifies map orientation. Ideal for children starting the sport. Is simple to use, having no moving parts. Is inexpensive.	Cannot be used to take a bearing. Can slip off the map and get lost.	Up to $15

EQUIPMENT TIP Consider buying both a thumb and protractor compass and practice using each at training sessions until you decide which suits you best.

Compass Types

Protractor Compass

The protractor compass is most familiar to newcomers to the sport, as it is used by hikers. This compass has a magnetic needle, a housing that can be rotated, a distance-measuring scale, and a direction-following arrow. If you buy a protractor compass, make sure it has a cord long enough to be attached to your wrist, even when you are laying it on your map to orient the map or take bearings. The cord ensures that you don't drop the compass and damage it as you run through the forest.

Thumb Compass

The thumb compass is an ingenious gadget that allows you to focus on the magnetic needle, quickly linking map north to magnetic north. The thumb compass attaches to the thumb and is kept on the map so that the map and compass are used as a single unit. It has a magnetic needle and a measuring scale but does not have rotating housing. Using the thumb compass to orient the map is very simple (see page 32 for orienting the map). You don't have to rotate the compass housing, as you do with a protractor compass, which saves you time. Thumb compasses are also less prone to error.

Clip Compass

A recent innovation that is proving to be an ideal starter compass for young children is the map guide or clip compass. This looks like a thumb compass but contains only a fixed housing and a magnetic needle. It is clipped onto the map rather than attached to the thumb. This is an advantage for those with small hands and encourages the map and compass to be used as a single unit.

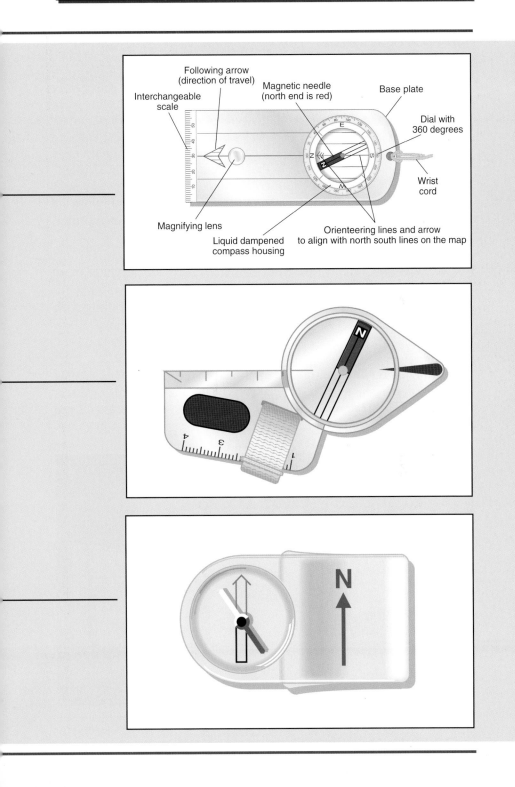

Following arrow
(direction of travel)

Magnetic needle
(north end is red)

Base plate

Interchangeable
scale

Dial with
360 degrees

Wrist
cord

Magnifying lens

Liquid dampened
compass housing

Orienteering lines and arrow
to align with north south lines on the map

Maps, Control Cards, and Description Sheets

Three pieces of necessary equipment that you'll receive when you register for a meet and pay your entry fee are a map, a control card, and a course description sheet. The orienteering map is the most important aid to navigation. It is often a work of art, and it is yours to keep when you have completed your course. Many experienced orienteers have acquired a large collection of maps as mementos of the different forests they have visited.

Control cards are carried by all competitors and are used by the meet organizers to check that each competitor has visited each control site on the course. Often a different colored card is used for each class of competitor.

EQUIPMENT TIP Control cards may be made of waterproof material. If yours is not, put it into a plastic bag before attaching it to your clothing with a safety pin.

Control descriptions are sometimes printed on the map, but just as often they are printed separately and handed out with the map. These descriptions tell you the exact features used at the control points and indicate the code number on the control.

© Brian Lochrin

Attaching the control card to your wrist and pinning the control description sheet to your sleeve helps you keep track of these important orienteering tools.

IMPORTANT ITEMS TO PACK FOR EACH MEET

Use this checklist to be sure you are well-equipped for every competition:

1. Your compass.
2. Polythene map cases to protect the map and control card (good quality 400-gauge plastic is best for clarity).
3. A selection of red pens that you'll use to copy the course from a master map to your own map (ball point pens, which don't stain in wet conditions, are best).
4. A whistle on a cord to use in case of emergency. Carry it pinned to a pocket.
5. Safety pins. You'll need at least four pins to attach your control card and description sheet to your clothing.
6. Insulation tape to secure your shoelaces. You will not want to stop to retie your shoes during the competition.
7. Sweatbands for your forehead and wrists in hot weather.
8. A basic first-aid kit including bandages, ointment, wraps, aspirin, and any special medications the participant uses.
9. Insect repellent and sunscreen that suits your skin type.
10. A high-energy snack. It can work wonders if you run out of energy during your course.
11. Your post-competition lunch and drink.

Consider keeping many of the smaller items in a plastic container and repack them after you have completed your run.

Buying Clothing and Equipment

You can find orienteering clothing and equipment at most specialist sports retailers, but I recommend checking out the goods that traders sell out of their cars at most meets. The larger meets and the orienteering festivals or multiday events usually have special areas reserved for retailers. Browsing through the latest clothing and equipment on sale is very much part of the attractive atmosphere of these large meets. It's fun to discuss bargains or possible purchases with fellow competitors before buying. The competition between retailers keeps prices low, and the retailers gain a reputation by offering greater choice, including clothing and equipment from around the world. Many retailers are active orienteers who manage to fit in their own run after servicing customers. A major advantage of buying from one of the specialist retailers is the opportunity to return faulty or unsuitable goods at the next meet, even though the goods have been used.

3

ORIENTEERING CORRECTLY

Your first orienteering competition is a special occasion—likely you'll be apprehensive but excited. Your objective is to navigate quickly and accurately to each of the controls on your course. Each control site is identified by a three-dimensional red and white, or orange and white, triangular marker. The marker's identification code corresponds to the appropriate control on your description list. It also has a punch with a distinctive pin pattern with which you will punch your control card.

It will be a big boost to your confidence if on your first time out you can complete the course without getting lost and collect all of the controls in the correct order in a reasonable time. So, with these goals in mind, let's look at ways to help you meet the challenges of the course. You'll need to learn race procedure, understand the key techniques of the sport, and be able to apply the techniques correctly.

Finding a control on the first try brings a big boost to your confidence as a beginner.

When You Arrive at a Meet

All meets provide in their pre-event advertising a time schedule for the competition. This schedule will tell you when you can register to compete (usually between 9:30 in the morning and 12:30 in the afternoon).

When you arrive at the competition site, you'll need to register for an appropriate course, so be sure to spend some time beforehand reading the notices and selecting a course that is technically easy and not too long. Likely you will choose one of the color-coded courses available. The events standards chart on the next page describes what the colors indicate.

Registering

Having chosen a course to enter, pay your entry fee and you'll be handed a map, a control card, and control descriptions for your chosen course. Normally, even on your first orienteering experience, you should find it easy to follow the correct procedure, as most meets have excellent signposting.

Control descriptions give you an exact description of the feature used at each control point. They also indicate the class you're running in, the length of the course, and, most important, the code number at each control.

COLOR-CODED EVENTS—STANDARDS FOR COMPETITORS AND PLANNERS

Color	Length (kilometers)	Control sites	Type of leg	Technical level	Time for most finishers (minutes)	Age
String	0.5-1.5	On the line		Easy	10-15	3+
White	1.0-1.5	Major line features and junctions	Line features, no route choice	Very easy	15-40	6-12
Yellow	1.0-2.5	Line features and very easy adjacent features	Line features, minimal route choice, no compass legs	Easy	20-45	8+ Beginners
Orange	2.0-3.5	Minor line and easy point features	Route choice, collecting features, near control	Medium	35-55	10+
Red	4.5-6.0			Medium	50-80	
Green	3.5-4.5	Small point and contour features	Fine compass and contours, more physical	Hard	35-55	
Blue	4.5-6.5			Hard	50-75	
Brown	6.5+			Hard	60-85	

TECHNIQUE TIP   Cover the control description sheet with plastic and secure it to your wrist with safety pins. (A sweatband on your wrist gives you something to pin the sheet to.) This will allow you to glance down at the description of the code and its number without stopping.

Your control card is a vital piece of evidence, proving that you have completed the course and visited each control site. At the start of the run, a race official will tear your control card's stub off the card and take it to the finish line, where it will be matched up again with the card when you have finished the course. If the control card is not waterproof, cover it with a plastic cover. Make a hole in the corner of the card and attach it to your wrist with a cord, or pin it securely to your arm or body, making sure that the boxes on the card are easy to punch. You'll punch each box on the card using the pin punches hanging at each control. Results officials will examine this series of pin punches at the finish of the race.

TECHNIQUE TIP   Copy the code numbers from the description sheet onto the control card boxes to allow easy checking at each control.

Allow at least 40 minutes after registering to get changed, make your way to the start, and warm up before setting off. Before leaving for the start, check that you have the correct competition clothing, that your shoelaces are taped, and that you're carrying a compass, control card, map case, pen and, if the meet demands it, a whistle.

At the Start

You'll need to arrive at the start (which will be well signposted) at least 10 minutes before your start time. This will allow you to synchronize your watch with the start clock and observe the start procedure. Watch what other competitors are doing. Look carefully at your map and try to locate the start position. If you can't do this by matching features on the ground, ask a fellow competitor.

Then spend a few minutes stretching and warming up (see chapter 4) to prepare your body for the race. When your time is called by a start official or displayed on a board, it's time for you to enter the starting box. At most meets you'll be called up 2 minutes before your actual start time and asked to step into the first row of the box. Standing alongside you will be a number of other competitors who have the same start time but are running different courses. Competitors in the same class as you and running the same course will have started 2 or 3 minutes before your time or at least 2 or 3 minutes after it. An official will move along the line of competitors, checking the control cards and collecting the stubs. The organizers use these stubs to check who is in the forest at any particular time. After your card is checked and your stub collected, move forward to the end of the first box to just behind the line of the second box. After 1 minute a buzzer will sound and you'll be asked to step forward into the next box.

© CompassSport/Hazelle Jackson

You'll need to copy the course onto your map at smaller meets.

▷─ GET READY TO START ─○────○────○────◎

In the minute before you start, try to relax. It helps if you look forward to the challenges ahead rather than worrying about your ability.

1. Re-examine your map. Check the contour lines on the map for the overall shape of the area. Is the course generally flat or hilly?

2. Check the scale of the map.

3. Identify line features—for example, trails, fences, walls, or streams.

4. Turn the map so that it is facing the same way as you are in the start lane and recheck the position of the start, both on your map and on the ground. A control marker will be placed in the terrain at the exact point shown by the triangle on your map.

From the start line is a good place to observe the direction in which other competitors first move into the forest. You are standing on the line and, with 10 seconds to go, the start official will ask you to step over the line and listen to a countdown. The buzzer will sound again, and from this point you are being timed.

Smaller meets may use master maps, which means you'll need to follow a tape to the maps and copy down a course onto your map. Using a red pen (a color not otherwise used on the orienteering map), copy the control circles onto your map. Be careful, as the center of each circle shows where the control marker is hanging in the forest. This will be your target. Take care to number the circles in order and link them with a continuous line. The finish will be shown by concentric circles. Place your map in its plastic cover and you're ready for the challenge ahead.

At this point, avoid the temptation to go running off into the forest after other competitors. Instead, fold your map so that only the area with the start and the first few controls is visible. The map will be easier to handle this way, and you can direct your attention to the precise area you're in.

Taking Off

Turn in the direction of the first control by orienting your map. Do this by holding the map so that it is completely aligned with the features on the ground. What you see on the left of the map should be on your left in the terrain, what you see on the right of the map should be on your right, and so on. The illustrations the next page show what you would see when looking at the highlighted sections of the map. An alternative is to use your compass to orient the map.

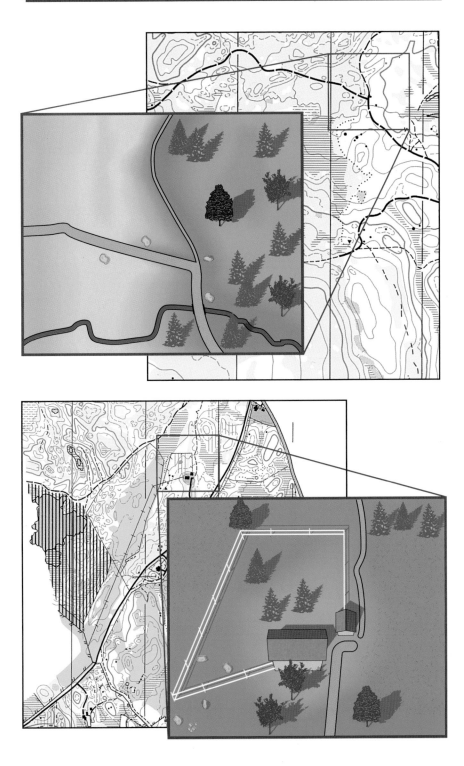

▷─ ORIENT THE MAP ─○─────○────○────◎

Lines running north on orienteering maps are magnetic. When these lines run parallel to the magnetic needle in the compass housing, your map is oriented.

1. Place the compass on the map with the long edge of the base plate parallel to the feature you want to follow. The direction-of-travel arrow on the base plate should point in the direction you want to go.

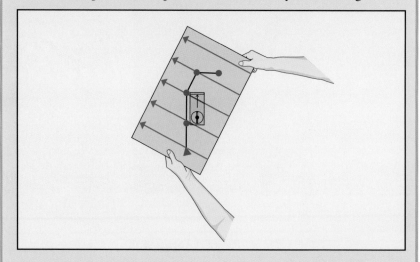

2. Turn yourself with map and compass together until the magnetic needle lies parallel with the north-south lines on the map. There's no need to turn the compass housing dial—just look at the needle. The map is now set and you are facing the direction you wish to travel.

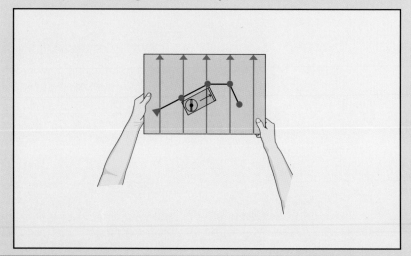

3. If you're using a thumb compass to set the map, fold the map square and small enough to "thumb" your position.

4. Hold the map so that you're looking straight along the route you want to take.

5. Place your thumb and the corner of the leading edge at your position. Use your other hand to hold the map steady.

6. With map and compass fixed in front of you, turn yourself until the magnetic needle lies parallel to the north-south lines on the map.

You have successfully oriented your map and are facing the direction you wish to travel.

With your map oriented, decide which features you want to follow to the first control and set off feeling confident.

At larger meets, maps are prepared with courses printed on them, so you won't need to copy your own course from a master map. The control descriptions are attached to the map and both are put in plastic covers. Instead of copying your map, you'll need to pick it up from a marked box after you've crossed the starting line.

Map Reading

The most fundamental technique of orienteering is reading the map. Orienteering maps are prepared (usually by orienteers) to show the exact shape of the ground. Using aerial photography, photogrammetry, and sophisticated survey techniques, the cartographer produces detailed and very accurate maps. The most important map feature, contour lines, will indicate the complexity of the land forms. Although some subjectivity is inevitable, good maps provide a picture of the ground that will help you make informed decisions about your direction of travel.

Orienteering maps are noted for the amount of detail they show, such as trails, streams, ditches, boulders, and cliffs. Orienteering maps are standardized throughout the world—all attempt to show the easiest way to travel over the terrain, indicating clearly the vegetation participants are likely to encounter.

Map Symbols and Scale

Maps are normally printed in five colors and contain a legend showing the meaning of the map's symbols. You'll soon become familiar with the most common symbols, especially if you think of the colors in conjunction with the symbol.

Recognizing Control Features

Quick and accurate map reading is essential to making correct route choices and recognizing control features. Each control flag on the course will be hanging on to, or placed very close to, a distinct feature clearly marked on the map. Knowing what to look for before you reach the control site saves you time and boosts your confidence. Carefully examine the following features, as you'll see all of them in your early orienteering experiences.

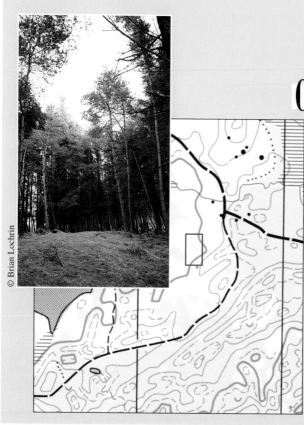

© Brian Lochrin

Clearings

The sun may shine more brilliantly through the trees in a clearing, so look up at the tree canopy rather than through the forest.

Marshes and Ponds

Look for the distinctive vegetation of these areas, such as reeds rather than water that may have dried up.

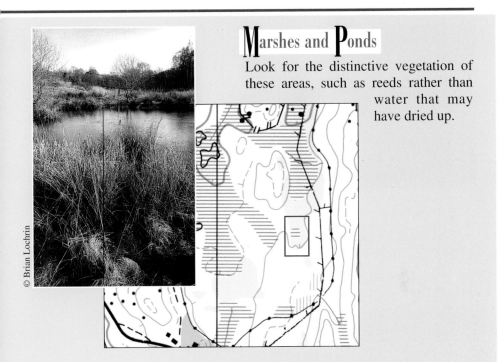

© Brian Lochrin

Knolls (small hills)

If the area is overgrown, look for normally low vegetation appearing higher up than usual. Lower branches on trees will also be higher than normal.

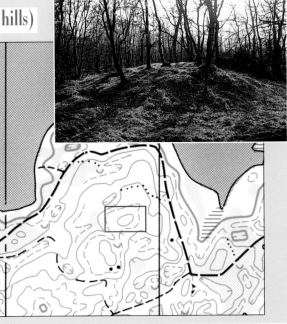

© Brian Lochrin

Depressions or Pits

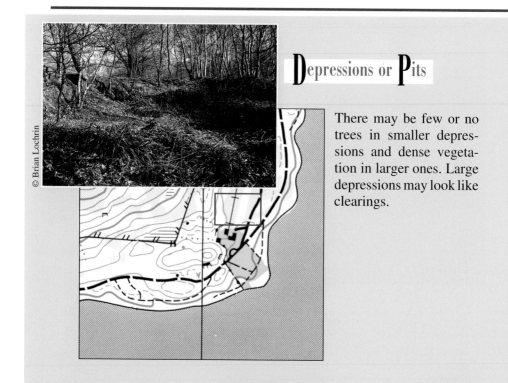

© Brian Lochrin

There may be few or no trees in smaller depressions and dense vegetation in larger ones. Large depressions may look like clearings.

Re-Entrants

These are shallow valleys. Controls are normally hung at the top end of the re-entrant unless otherwise noted on the control description. Look for ground falling away.

© Brian Lochrin

Walls and Fences

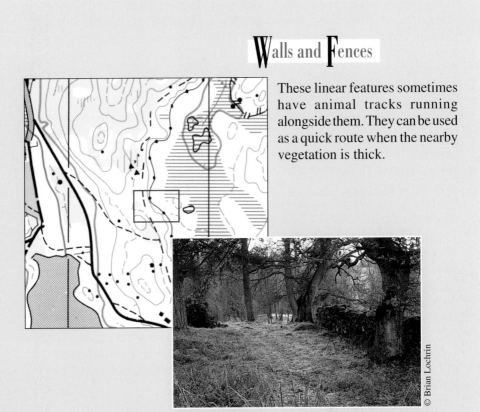

These linear features sometimes have animal tracks running alongside them. They can be used as a quick route when the nearby vegetation is thick.

© Brian Lochrin

Black symbols generally show man-made features such as trails, walls, buildings, and fences, and natural features such as cliffs or boulders. Blue symbols indicate water features, such as lakes, streams, ditches or marshes. Brown symbols, the most difficult to master, show contour lines (map lines that show all the land of the same height), gullies, earth banks, or knolls. Yellow shows vegetation and indicates land that is relatively quick to travel over, such as open fields or moorland. Green also shows vegetation. The darker the green, the slower you'll likely progress through the terrain. The white on the map, often the predominant area, indicates runable forest. Orienteering maps always have magnetic north lines printed on them. This is very helpful to you as you can ignore the magnetic variation when using your compass.

Make sure you know the scale of the map before you compete to determine the distance you cover on your way around the course. The most common scales used in the sport are 1:10,000 or 1:15,000. A scale of 1:5,000 or even 1:7,500 may be used for a smaller map of school grounds or a town park, for example. The majority of meets provide a 1:15,000 map, which is sometimes enlarged to 1:10,000 for older or younger competitors, who find the larger map clearer. You should get to know how far 50 and 100 meters appear on maps of differing scales.

On a 1:10,000 map, 1 millimeter equals 10 centimeters on the ground, and 1 centimeter equals 100 meters on the ground. On a 1:15,000 map, 1 millimeter equals 15 meters on the ground, and 1 centimeter equals 150 meters on the ground.

Be sure to study the scale of the map and to identify prominent features to give yourself a head start on the course.

Understanding Contours

Knolls, re-entrants, spurs, and depressions are shown on the map as contour lines. You will rarely move around a course without having to make sense of contours. A map is a two-dimensional representation of a three-dimensional area, and cartographers use contouring to indicate height or depth. Contour lines enable you to visualize the shape of the ground from the map.

Contour awareness will affect your route choice. Features such as ridges or valleys are permanent, so you can use them to guide you into a control. Ridges and valleys are often used as control sites themselves, and you'll need to learn to recognize them on your map.

UNDERSTANDING CONTOURS

Contours are lines on the map that join together points on the ground of equal height. They are usually drawn at 5-meter intervals and enable you to visualize the shape of the ground. The closer the contour lines to each other, the steeper the slope of the ground.

Visualizing Dimension

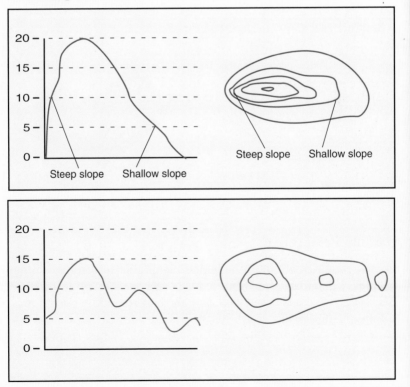

Reading the Shape of the Ground

Once you can recognize contours, the shape of the ground will be clear to you as you look at your map. Re-entrants, spurs, knolls, and depressions occur frequently in orienteering and are often used as control sites. Learning how to read a contour map quickly and recognizing the shape of the ground will help you become a better orienteer.

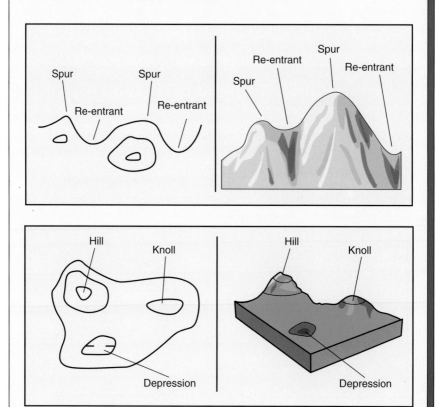

Gaining Perspective

Contour features are often huge and being able to distinguish these features will affect your route choice and success as an orienteer. Because the event is timed, choosing the best route for your skills and abilities is important.

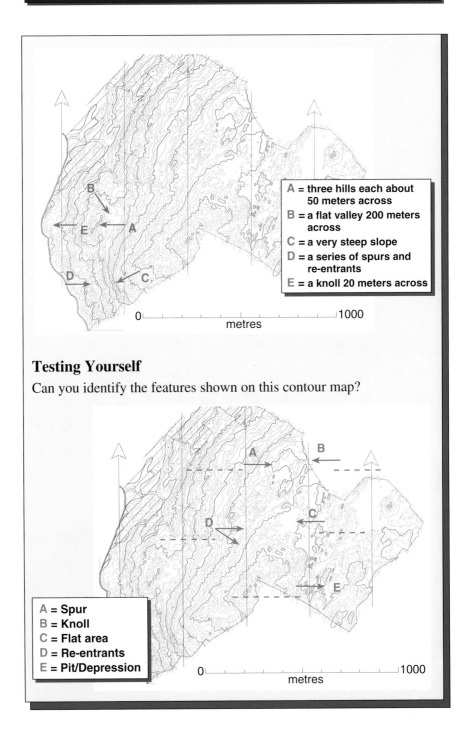

A = three hills each about 50 meters across
B = a flat valley 200 meters across
C = a very steep slope
D = a series of spurs and re-entrants
E = a knoll 20 meters across

0 |_____| 1000
metres

Testing Yourself

Can you identify the features shown on this contour map?

A = Spur
B = Knoll
C = Flat area
D = Re-entrants
E = Pit/Depression

0 |_____| 1000
metres

Running the Course

Your success on a course depends on how well you use key techniques. Let's take a turn around a short course designed to illustrate these techniques.

Complete Course

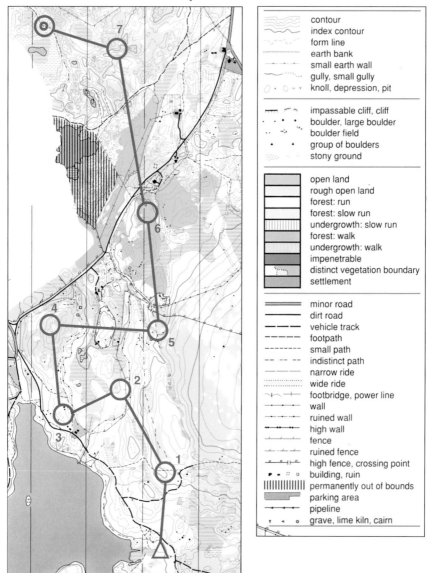

	contour
	index contour
	form line
	earth bank
	small earth wall
	gully, small gully
	knoll, depression, pit
	impassable cliff, cliff
	boulder, large boulder
	boulder field
	group of boulders
	stony ground
	open land
	rough open land
	forest: run
	forest: slow run
	undergrowth: slow run
	forest: walk
	undergrowth: walk
	impenetrable
	distinct vegetation boundary
	settlement
	minor road
	dirt road
	vehicle track
	footpath
	small path
	indistinct path
	narrow ride
	wide ride
	footbridge, power line
	wall
	ruined wall
	high wall
	fence
	ruined fence
	high fence, crossing point
	building, ruin
	permanently out of bounds
	parking area
	pipeline
	grave, lime kiln, cairn

Starting the Course

It's important to set off in the right direction, so never rush away from the start or, even worse, follow other competitors. The first control is often the key to the whole course, so the time you spend thinking now will be well spent. The first control on your course is described as a depression, and you must plan a route toward it.

Start to Control 1

Following Handrails

If you examine the map carefully, you'll see a succession of features that you can follow right up to the control. In this case a stream, small trail, vehicle track, and another trail lead directly to the control site. This may not be the fastest or the shortest route, but it is the safest and will ensure that you get off to a good start. The key technique we're working here is called "following handrails." It is a technique that all beginners must master. Linear features such as streams, fences, trails, and walls make excellent handrails and offer sure and fast routes, even if they involve greater distances. Using handrails at the start of the course builds confidence, allows you to read your map on the run, and helps you become familiar with the map without looking down at your feet all the time.

TECHNIQUE TIP   Always plan your route carefully to the first control, select a safe route, and execute the leg steadily, keeping in map contact all the time. It will help if you have your map oriented when you read it, keep it folded, and try to thumb your position along the map as you move through the terrain.

You have reached the first control site successfully and achieved your first goal. Now you have two important tasks to complete before you move on to the next control. First, check the code attached to the orienteering flag to make sure it matches the code on your control description sheet. If it does not, you are not at the correct control site. If it does match, complete your second task by marking your control card with the punch hanging on or near the flag. The punch mark must be imprinted in the correct box on your card (in this case, in the box marked "1"). Officials will later check your card to

Control 1 to Control 2

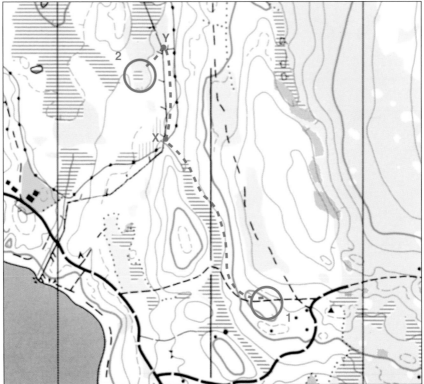

see if you have the correct imprint in each box—this is the only evidence that you have visited each of the control sites.

Having successfully reached the first control, checked the code, and punched your control card, you now have to plan the route to the next control. Be careful—after punching your control card, it's possible to get disoriented and leave the control in the wrong direction. Orient your map, identify control 2, and plan your best route.

Don't ever leave a control site without knowing how you're going to navigate to the next point. Most errors arise when competitors run off without thinking the leg through. Avoid mistakes by always knowing where you are and where you want to go. You should always have a plan in mind.

Choosing an Attack Point

The control description for control 2 is a marsh, and the control is in a rather featureless semi-open area. Once again, handrails are available, in this case a small trail, a linear marsh, a stream, and a fence.

This leg gives you the opportunity to use another key technique: choosing an attack point. Attack points are distinct features close to the control that are quicker and easier to locate than the control may be. They are often on handrails. On this leg to control 2 there are two possible attack points: X, the stream junction, and Y, the fence junction. Y is closer to the control but entails traveling further. X is farther from the control but avoids turning back after passing the control. At your stage, you should choose Y, the attack point closest to the control, as this will mean traveling a shorter distance while moving slowly. Using an attack point will enable you to move at speed, taking advantage of your handrails. Orienteers call this "rough orienteering"— not all the details on the map are used, only the major features.

Fine Orienteering

Once you've reached an attack point, you'll need to slow down and use another technique called "fine orienteering." This involves studying the map carefully and taking in all the fine detail. Your aim is to have a complete picture of the terrain. When fine orienteering you should use a compass bearing.

TECHNIQUE TIP   When using handrails, practice reading the map on the run. Obviously, the more you stop to read the map, the longer you'll take to complete the course. Always match your running speed to the complexity of the map and terrain.

Taking a Bearing

The final section of the leg requires two more techniques: using your compass and judging distance. You'll need to use these techniques again as you move between legs 2 and 3. Use your compass to orient the map (see page 32) and to take a bearing. Taking a bearing from the map is an accurate way of determining the direction to travel.

Control 2 to Control 3

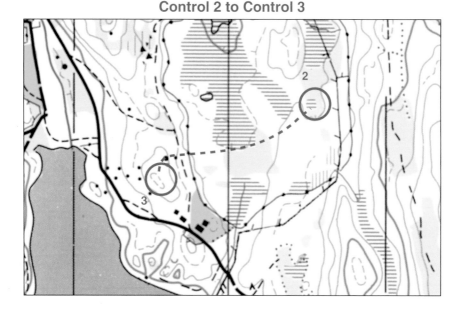

Place your compass on the map so that its edge parallels the feature you wish to follow (or the line of travel you want to take). Turn the dial until north (N) on the compass housing points to map north and the red lines in the compass housing are parallel to the N/S lines on the map. Holding the compass flat and straight in front of you, turn your body with the map and compass together until the needle lies along the north-south line in the housing. You should now be facing your direction of travel.

Judging Distance

If you examine leg 2-3, you'll see how carefully you must use your compass to ensure that you're traveling in the right direction upon leaving the control. The control site for this leg is a knoll in an area of woodland contained between a wall and a dirt road. The best route to this control is to run straight on a bearing, passing the tips of the marsh and crossing the wall, and possibly using the two boulders at the foot of the hill to determine your exact location. You should estimate the distance from the wall to the hill top (about 60 meters).

The best way to judge distance is to know how many paces you take to progress 100 meters. It is easier to count double paces (i.e., every time either your left or right foot strikes the ground). You'll need to factor in the gradient and the type of terrain you're running over, but as a rule an adult travels between 40 and 50 double paces over 100 meters. Once you know how many paces equal a meter, you can measure distances on your map using the map scale and the interchangeable scale found on your compass.

TECHNIQUE TIP   Try to master pace counting. Counting paces takes no extra time during competition, and it may help save time by keeping you from stopping either well short of or well beyond the control.

Choosing the Best Route

Courses are planned to test a competitor's level of skill and fitness. A good course planner will frequently test decision making by providing a choice of routes between controls. Route choice is the essence of orienteering; choosing the fastest route and completing it successfully are the keys to winning competitions.

BASIC PRINCIPLES OF ROUTE CHOICE

When assessing a leg, the last part is more important than the beginning, as it is essential to examine the optimal line into the control and then plan a route back from it. Your route choice should be guided by the availability of a suitable attack point. No matter how many choices are available, on most occasions the time difference between alternative routes will be small; it is the execution of the route taken that is the vital factor. If you have to decide between a longer route over flat ground and a shorter one uphill, your state of fitness will guide you.

The route you choose should reflect your strengths and weaknesses. If you can run quickly but are weak technically, you're better off choosing a route with many handrails.

The next leg, from control 3 to 4, involves three possible choices of route: A, B, and C. Route A is the longest but offers use of a dirt road and an opportunity to run faster. If you choose this route, you will need to choose an attack point carefully. The point where the earth bank meets the dirt road might be where you should leave the road and start climbing up to the northmost hill top.

Control 3 to Control 4

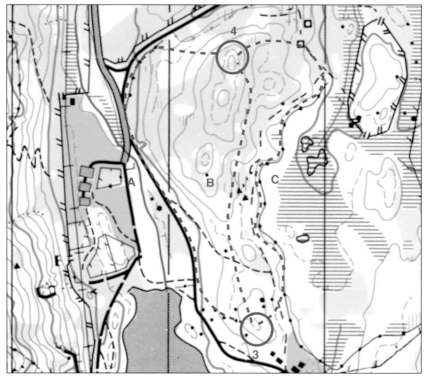

Route C also makes use of a handrail, in this case a wall or the indistinct trail. The southmost ruin is an obvious attack point that could lead you to the spur east of the control and then on to the control site itself.

The experienced orienteer would probably choose route B. It is the shortest, most direct route and, although no handrail is available, the long twin-peaked hill is a landmark that could be used to this effect. The shallow re-entrant on the right of the marked route is a suitable attack point.

Since at this stage your main objective is to minimize errors, route C would probably be your best choice. This route keeps you from losing height and having to climb again, as you would if you chose route A.

Collecting Features

The next leg on this short course (to control 5) gives you the opportunity to use two more techniques: collecting features and aiming off.

Collecting features are long or large features that can be used as checking features en route and also to stop you from overshooting the control. On this leg, the collecting features on the chosen route are:

A—an indistinct trail,

B—a stream in a narrow marsh,

C—a fence,

D—a wall,

E—a narrow marsh, and

F—an indistinct trail on the edge of the wood.

The final feature, F, acts as a collector that ensures you don't overshoot the control site.

Use collecting features whenever you can to confirm your location on the map as you travel across the terrain. On the chosen route for this leg if you are off line, you will be stopped by the indistinct trail and the open terrain and avoid overshooting the control site.

Control 4 to Control 5

On a leg such as this, when you know that you'll be stopped by a collector, you can save time at the control site by choosing the direction you'll take from the control before you get there. You can save even more time by glancing at the control code number on your description sheet as you run toward the control.

Aiming Off

When you reach the marsh, if the control is not in front of you, is it to the left or the right? Time could be wasted finding out. You can eliminate the risk of wasting time by deliberately aiming to one side of the control, and you will then know which way to turn to reach it. This technique is called "aiming off."

Refining Your Skills

On the next leg of the course (to control 6), if you wish to travel in a straight line (i.e., the shortest, most direct route), you will run through an open well-contoured area. Careful scrutiny of the map reveals the control site to be a re-entrant on the edge of two small knolls. Following the route shown will involve passing between two hills, dropping down and past a small knoll, then proceeding between the next two knolls into the re-entrant.

Control 5 to Control 6

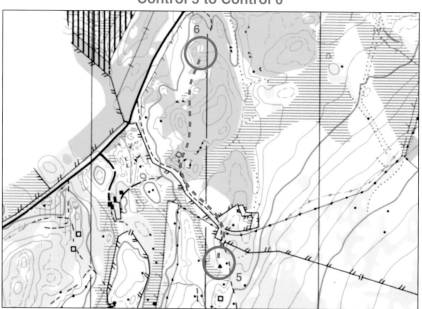

Learning to Relocate

The next leg of the course (to control 7) is the most difficult in that the control is a small spur in an undulating semi-open area. The area has few handrails and no obvious attack point.

Control 6 to Control 7

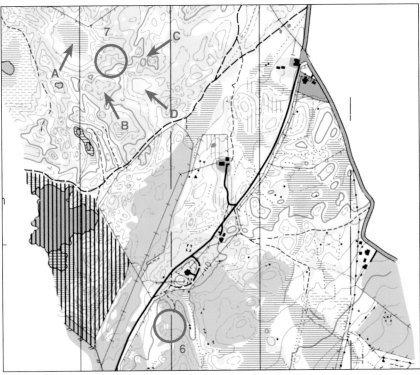

 **TECHNIQUE TIP**   Mistakes often occur, particularly in technically difficult areas, when you are put off by other competitors. Try to ignore everyone else on the course and concentrate on your own map reading and decision making.

After crossing the trail running northeast-southwest, you'll have to pace count and read the contours carefully to ensure that you don't lose contact with the map and run around aimlessly, hoping to find the control site by luck. If you become unsure of your position on the map, several prominent features not far from the control site can help you relocate:

A—the large marsh,

B—the depressions southwest of the control site,

C—three depressions east of the control site, or

D—the flat-topped hill, where the undergrowth is described as slow run.

If you are unfortunate and become completely lost, don't get down on yourself. Most beginners to the sport lose their way some time, as do a good many experienced orienteers. If you get lost, don't panic and wander aimlessly, hoping something will turn up. Resist the temptation to follow other competitors, however competent they look. They are likely on a different course, and following them will only make your situation worse. An alternative is to examine the possibility that you left the last control 180 degrees in the wrong direction (a common error). If this is a possibility, the solution is to retrace your steps to the point where you last had map contact. If it was the previous control, return to it and start the leg again.

▷─FIND YOUR WAY ─O────O────O────◎

If you lose your way, a clear head and some methodical planning will help you reduce your anxiety and relocate.

1. Stop running; while standing still, try to orient the map using your compass.

2. Examine the map and try to match it to the surrounding terrain.

3. Look around for large clear features you can confidently identify on the ground and try to match them to your map. What is the relationship of these large features to smaller features?

4. If things don't match, try to remember where you were on the map the last time you were certain of your position. Stopping to read the map carefully and weigh your options clearly is often enough to allow you to relocate and start your route again.

5. However, if you're still lost, look for a large line feature such as a field edge, a road, or a stream nearest to the area of the map that you think you're in. Using your compass, head out for this spot. It should be much easier to follow the line feature until it crosses another feature that you can recognize, and you can then precisely relocate.

If you become distressed or cold and are not enjoying the experience as a beginner, it's quite all right to ask a fellow competitor to show you where you are on the map or point you back to the finish. Only do this when it is really necessary, as stopping people will usually break their concentration.

Finishing the Course

The final leg of the course (from control 7 to the finish) is straightforward. It requires you to take a bearing on leaving the control site before moving south of the marsh as quickly as possible until you hit the trail. Then simply follow the trail northwest until you reach the finish.

At the last control you'll often find streamers marking the way to the finish line. Keep moving until you have reached the end of the streamers and until you have crossed the line, as you are still being timed. Just after crossing the line you'll be asked to unpin your control card and give it to an official.

It is important that you report to the finish at every meet, even if you don't complete the course. If you don't hand in your control card, the organizers

Control 7 to Finish

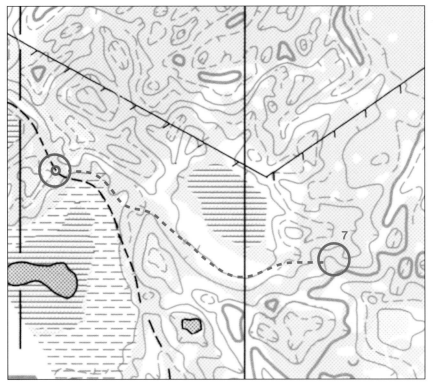

will not be able to match it to the stub you handed to the start official and will assume that you are still out in the forest when the meet is over.

Within minutes after you've crossed the finish line, your time and current position in the race will be calculated, and the organizers will display results.

The finish!

On Your Own

Now it's time to find out whether you're ready to orienteer on your own. Examine the course on the next page and plan your way around it. Note the techniques you'll need on each leg and compare your route with that on page 56.

Practice Course

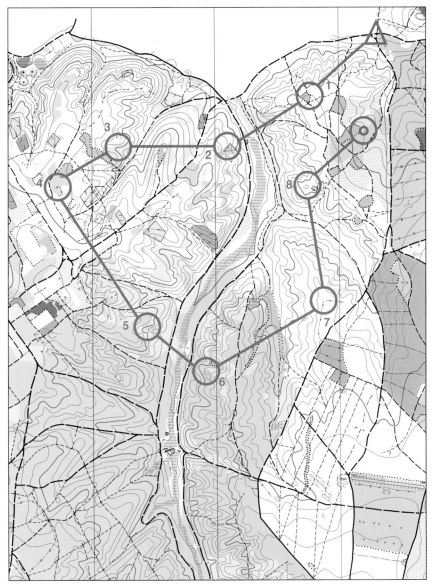

Completed Course

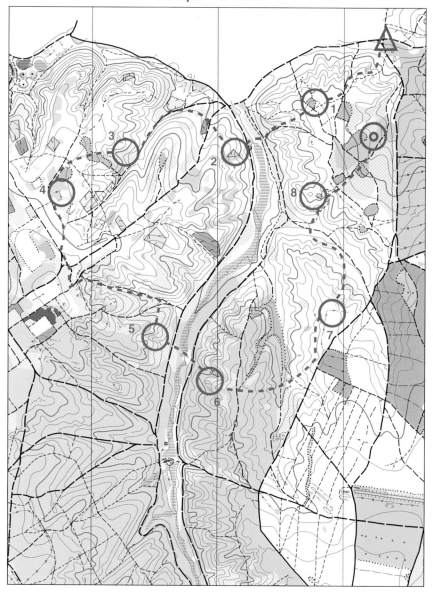

4

ORIENTEERING FITNESS AND SAFETY

Orienteering involves coordinating mental skills with physical activity. One of the main attractions of the sport is it challenges both the mind and body. Over the last two decades, many people have recognized the link of regular exercise to physical fitness and healthy living. With health-related physical fitness the priority it is in today's society, you may be attracted to orienteering because of its emphasis on running and its healthy outdoor image.

As a newcomer, your main objective in orienteering may be to complete courses without making too many mistakes. The time factor is less important, as you are now focusing on correct technique and eliminating technical weaknesses. However, you'll soon become aware of how long it takes other people in your age group to complete the course, and you may wonder about your own fitness for orienteering. You cannot enjoy the sport to the fullest if your body is not able to cope with the demands of running around the course.

Improving your physical fitness will help you run courses faster.

An orienteering competition involves running across country with short pauses. As a beginner, you may need to run from 30 minutes up to an hour. Lack of conditioning should not prevent you from starting the sport and getting satisfaction from meeting the mental demands that the course planner sets. Though completing courses at even a walking pace will improve your conditioning a little, adequate training will lead to faster times, a feeling of success, and the motivation to keep improving. The fitter you are, the more you'll enjoy orienteering.

The major component of fitness for orienteering is known as cardiorespiratory endurance or, more simply, stamina. This is the heart's ability to pump blood and deliver oxygen to the working muscles. You will also need some muscular strength, especially in your legs, which will need to carry you over rough, sometimes hilly terrain. Muscular strength must be accompanied by some muscular endurance, as you'll be competing for at least 30-minute periods as a beginner, and longer as you become more experienced.

The third component of orienteering fitness is flexibility—your muscles must be able to stretch without pain over a wide range of movements. You can benefit both your course times and your general health by analyzing your level of fitness and beginning a training program.

Are You Ready to Compete?

If you participate in other recreational sports, you already have an idea of what kind of shape you're in. However, before increasing training or taking part in any extensive physical activity, you need to consider your current state of health. The older you are, the truer this is. If you're concerned in any way about your present health, seek a medical okay before starting a training program or running your first course.

If you participate regularly in active sports such as football, track and field, or tennis, or if you cross-country ski, swim, or cycle, you'll be able to cope quite well with the demands of an orienteering course. If you think of yourself as active but don't regularly sustain exercise for 30 minutes or more, determine your cardiorespiratory fitness by trying the 1-mile run test, a reliable and valid measure of cardiorespiratory fitness. This test requires no equipment and little preparation. Simply select a 400-meter track or other flat area where you can measure 1 mile. When you take the test, keep in mind that four factors outside your level of fitness may affect your performance:

- The air temperature. It should not be too hot or cold when you run.
- The running surface. It should be firm and dry.
- The wind. Light or no wind is preferable.
- Your familiarity with the test. You need to know how to pace yourself to avoid tiring out early in the test.

Most people can gauge pace judgment after just one or two practice trials. Be sure to warm up thoroughly before taking the test or running a practice trial.

Norms for this test are available. The tables on the next page have been adapted for children or adults about to begin orienteering.

If you fall in the first two categories on these tables, consider running courses no longer than 3 kilometers. Gradually increase your physical activity to improve your cardiovascular endurance.

Even if you perform well in the test, you'll want to improve your general fitness. Regular participation in orienteering will help, as will a physical training program.

MEN'S AEROBIC FITNESS CLASSIFICATION. ONE MILE RUN/WALK

Rating	Age group/Time in minutes:seconds						Action
	13-19 yrs	20-29 yrs	30-39 yrs	40-49 yrs	50-59 yrs	60+ yrs	
Very poor	>10:20	>10:40	>10:50	>11:30	>11:40	>13:10	Walk around the course
Poor	8:07-10:20	9:20-10:40	9:35-10:50	10:24-11:30	11:20-11:40	12:40-13:10	Walk around the course
Fair	6:56-8:06	8:00-9:19	8:10-9:34	8:40-10:23	9:40-11:19	10:56-12:39	Compete
Good	6:26-6:55	7:11-7:59	7:21-8:09	7:40-8:39	8:20-9:39	9:20-10:55	Compete
Excellent	5:42-6:25	6:30-7:10	6:40-7:20	6:50-7:39	7:20-8:19	7:30-9:19	Compete

WOMEN'S AEROBIC FITNESS CLASSIFICATION. ONE MILE RUN/WALK

Rating	Age group/Time in minutes:seconds						Action
	13-19 yrs	20-29 yrs	30-39 yrs	40-49 yrs	50-59 yrs	60+ yrs	
Very poor	>12:20	>12:40	>13:00	>13:20	>13:40	>14:00	Walk around the course
Poor	11:18-12:20	12:20-12:40	12:40-13:00	13:00-13:20	13:20-13:40	13:40-14:00	Walk around the course
Fair	9:40-11:17	10:40-12:19	11:00-12:39	11:40-12:59	11:40-13:19	12:40-13:39	Compete
Good	8:20-9:39	9:00-10:39	9:40-10:59	10:40-11:39	11:00-11:39	11:40-12:39	Compete
Excellent	8:00-8:19	8:20-8:59	8:40-9:39	9:10-10:39	9:40-10:59	11:00-11:39	Compete

Warming Up and Stretching Before Exercise

Establish a warm-up routine before doing any vigorous exercise. Warm-up should consist of general loosening up, walking or jogging, and static stretching. Work particularly on the parts of your body most vulnerable to injury and at risk when orienteering—your ankles, legs, knees, hips, and back.

Loosening Up

Spend 5 to 10 minutes gradually mobilizing your joints and encouraging your muscles to work, especially if you're cold or have been sitting in a car. All movements should be slow and controlled at a rate of one repetition each second. Perform each rotation at least five times in each direction. Gently ease each joint through its maximum range of movement.

ANKLE ROTATION Slowly circle one foot clockwise and then repeat the movement counterclockwise. Repeat the process using your other leg. You can do this exercise either seated or standing up.

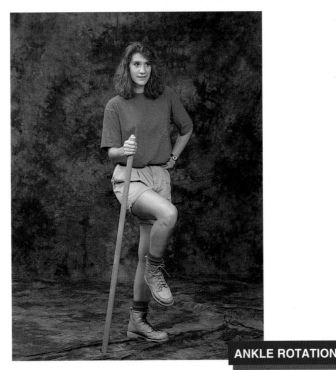

ANKLE ROTATION

HIP ROTATION   Stand on one leg with support. Slowly rotate your raised leg by moving your knee inward, then away. Make the movement a large arc. Repeat in both directions and with both legs.

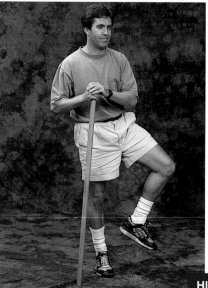

HIP ROTATION

SPINAL ROTATION   Stand with feet about shoulder-width apart. Slowly twist your upper body to the right and then to the left. Keep your hips facing forward and your heels on the ground. Repeat in both directions.

SPINAL ROTATION

HEEL RAISES   With feet shoulder-width apart, alternately raise and lower your heels. Keep the balls of both feet in contact with the ground. Gradually increase the speed at which you alternate heels and start a jogging motion. Keep this up for 30 seconds.

HEEL RAISES

Walking and Jogging

At this point you should attempt to gradually raise your heart rate, increase blood flow to your muscles, and raise your body temperature by walking and jogging. You can do this on the way to the course if you have the opportunity. Be sure to gradually increase from walk, to brisk walk, to jog. You should not be running at race speed during this phase.

Static Stretching

This should be the last thing you do before you start, and it should be automatic. Don't arrive at the start late, with too little time to do your static stretching.

Your aim in this phase is to gently stretch your muscles and remove the tightness. Your body must be ready to stretch as you run the course or you may incur injury. Stretching thoroughly before physical activity greatly reduces the risk of injury. When stretching, move slowly to a full stretch and don't jerk. If you can, hold the stretch for up to 30 seconds. Never stretch so far that you feel pain, and be sure to avoid bouncing—it can lead to a muscle or joint injury.

TRAINING TIP Stretch your muscles to remove tightness before exercise and again afterward to cool down. Try to make stretching a daily routine whether you exercise or not.

CALF STRETCH Lean on a support with your front foot about 45 centimeters from the support and your rear foot 60 centimeters further back. Keep your back straight and move your hips forward until you feel very slight discomfort in your calf. Hold, then slowly return to starting point. Repeat on both legs.

CALF STRETCH

HIP STRETCH   Support your weight using your hands and arms. Move your left leg forward until your knee is directly over your ankle. The knee of your right leg should rest on the ground. Keeping both knees in the same position, move the front of your hip down and hold; then slowly return to the starting position. Repeat. Do the same with your right leg forward.

HIP STRETCH

HAMSTRING STRETCH   Sit on the ground and extend your right leg. Rest the sole of your left foot against your extended right leg. Keep your right foot at right angles to the ground. Hold onto your right leg near your ankle, bend forward from your hips, but keep your back straight until you feel the stretch at the back of your thigh. Hold, then slowly return to the starting position. Repeat. Do the same with your left leg. Always bend from your hips and keep your back straight.

HAMSTRING STRETCH

HIP FLEXOR STRETCH   Kneeling on one knee, move your hips forward slowly until you feel a stretch in the front thigh of your back leg. Keep your front knee over your front foot. Hold and repeat.

HIP FLEXOR STRETCH

QUADRICEPS STRETCH   Standing on one leg, bend the knee of your other leg and grasp your ankle with one hand. Do not lean forward. Hold your foot close to your buttocks, making sure your knee is correctly aligned and not twisted. Repeat with your other leg.

QUADRICEPS STRETCH

A Guide to Improving Fitness

Orienteering regularly will improve your physical fitness, but if you want optimal benefit, you should exercise regularly, at least three times per week. Most orienteers train by running, preferably in the forest or over grass rather than roads. You'll benefit by gradually increasing the distance you can run and the speed you generate. If you can complete your course without having to stop and rest, you're on your way to successful orienteering. Running distances will obviously strengthen your leg muscles, but supplemental leg exercises will help, especially for uphill sections.

So you can fully concentrate on navigation, you should be able to run around the course without thinking about the effort involved. This will mean repeatedly running quite quickly for short distances (100 to 400 meters), with short recovery periods. Ideally, your fitness level will allow you to run comfortably over rough terrain and up, down, and sometimes across slopes.

As nice as it would be to become fit overnight, it's important to remember that it doesn't work this way. So, don't rush things. If you're not at your top fitness level, it doesn't mean you're not ready to orienteer. One of the best things about our sport is you can do it at your own speed. It has been my experience that as you learn to love orienteering, you naturally want to get better at it, which involves becoming more fit. Usually, the two feed each other: The fitter you are, the more you enjoy orienteering, and the more you enjoy orienteering, the fitter you become.

Avoiding and Coping With Injury

Orienteering is a safe sport, but injuries do occur. Knowing this, we can try to minimize their frequency and severity. Orienteering injuries fall into two broad categories: traumatic and overuse.

Traumatic orienteering injuries occur suddenly, usually as a result of a specific incident. They include sprained ankles, pulled muscles, bruises, and joint injuries. These injuries are usually caused by overstretching a muscle, twisting a joint, or falling over.

Overuse injuries are unlikely to affect beginners, as such injuries develop over time. They are caused by repetitive actions that result in a body part being overstressed. Factors that contribute to overuse injuries include using worn or poor-fitting footwear, suddenly increasing the number of miles you run, or changing the terrain you run over. Needless to say, if you feel pain in any area, seek medical advice before continuing activity that involves this area.

BUILDING UP A TRAINING PROGRAM

We train to become fit enough to compete and to reach our potential in our sport. Any training program should include some slow, long runs (more than 45 minutes). Such runs are socially and psychologically reassuring. If you frequently run for as long as it normally takes to complete a course, you will improve your fitness and find yourself able to run faster. Try to include some running up and down slopes, as you'll almost certainly encounter hills on your course, and you'll get a tremendous boost from running (albeit slowly) all the way up the slope. This type of training produces dramatic improvement in your cardio-vascular endurance.

Fartlek training—a mixture of fast running for short distances with recovery periods where you slowly jog—simulates an orienteering race and, if done with a partner, can be fun. Don't neglect training in spells of cold, inclement weather. Instead, find a gym and start circuit training. This will help you build up specific muscle groups, become more flexible, and add protection against injury.

Prevention of injury is better than trying to cure a problem. If you're not used to exercise, avoid trying too much too soon. Increase the load on your body gradually. Start with a training program that involves slow, steady runs over short distances (less than a mile). A little training frequently is more beneficial than a lot suddenly. A short run every other day will provide a fitness base for your body. Gradually increase the distance you run, then the speed, but stay within your comfort zone. You'll eventually manage to run further with less effort.

Whenever you train, wear footwear appropriate for your running style. A knowledgeable specialist retailer of running shoes will fit you correctly and tell you what type of shoes suit your physique and style. If the retailer does not ask you to try the shoes on and then watch you run in the shop, go somewhere else to buy your shoes.

One cause of injury in orienteering is the tendency of beginners to stop frequently when competing. If the weather is cold or wet, your body cools down quickly and is at risk when you start running again. Always wear appropriate orienteering clothing (see pages 16-18), including full leg cover and gaiters.

Of course, even the best precautions can't prevent all injuries. The best rule is when you feel pain, stop running. Your body is warning you that something is wrong. Seek medical advice as soon as possible—within hours, not days. If you can tell from the pain that you have pulled a muscle or a tendon or that you have somehow damaged a joint, apply a fresh cold pack to the injury every few hours. It also helps if you elevate and compress the injured part of the body.

INJURY PREVENTION TIP

Traumatic and overuse injuries are more likely if your body is not physically ready. Always warm up thoroughly before exercising.

Eventually, after treatment and rest, any injury you sustain will clear up and you'll be tempted to begin training or competing again. Take great care when recovering from an injury. Start back slowly, and gradually build up your exercise program. Avoid taking pain killers to run. They mask the pain and allow you, in the short term, to compete when you are unfit, which often results in further injury. You might turn what could have been a slight injury into a severe one.

Staying Safe

As we've mentioned, injuries in orienteering are rare, and if you do happen to hurt yourself, there are many competitors in the forest to stop and help you if you blow your whistle. If you feel you're in danger because you cannot relocate or you have injured yourself, use the emergency signal: six long blasts on your whistle, then repeating them 30 seconds later. When you hear the rescue reply of three short blasts, respond with six again until you are found.

Course planners build safety into courses and mark boundaries that are unsafe to cross. Planners tape any especially hazardous features, such as high cliffs and swiftly flowing streams. If competitors have to cross obstacles, high fences, or water, crossing points are usually provided. Brightly colored tape is used to steer competitors to the crossing points, which are clearly marked on the map with a red X.

Be sure to use official crossing points when you're instructed to do so. At most meets, competitors who ignore this instruction are disqualified, as they may put themselves or others at risk. Areas out of bounds are always no go for competitors. These areas may be off limits because the landowner does not want them to be crossed—or they may well contain dangerous terrain that puts you at risk.

© CompassSport/Ned Paul

Don't cross the brightly colored tape that signals hazardous features.

Full arm and leg cover, including gaiters, provide some protection from thorns or plants such as poison oak, but it is best to stay well clear. Often areas with poisonous plants will be shut off with tape, but you should learn to recognize these plants, just in case.

Animals rarely cause a problem for orienteers, as meet officials avoid terrain where dangerous animals may live, but do always keep an eye open for snakes. If you do see a snake, particularly in the vicinity of a control or crossing point, report this to an official at the finish.

SAFETY TIP   Slow down and watch where you put your feet whenever you cross rocky ground, especially in wet weather.

If the temperature is high or conditions humid, you may be tempted to drink from a stream. Resist this temptation, as the water may be polluted or contain harmful bacteria such as Giardia. In hot weather, meet organizers provide drink stations at suitable places around the course. Take advantage of these, as it is important that you replace the water you lose through sweating. If you become thirsty or short of breath, or if you feel dizzy or confused, drink water immediately. You may be dehydrated.

Even in moderate temperatures, your body loses three or more quarts of water every 24 hours through perspiration and urination. During exercise this loss increases. Drink more than you think you need (enough to keep your urine light).

Although most orienteering occurs under the tree canopy, in hot and sunny weather you risk getting sunburned, especially on your head and face. Take special care if you are fair skinned or competing at high elevations, where fewer ultraviolet rays are naturally blocked. Before competing, cover exposed parts of your body with a sunscreen that has a protection factor of 15 or more.

Some days you may need a cap for protection against cold or wind, so it's a good idea to bring one along. Also, wearing a sweatband around your forehead will help keep sweat out of your eyes. You'll have a happier orienteering experience if you're protected against cold, wind, rain, and strong sunshine.

The Country Code

Much orienteering is done on private land or national forest parks in areas that are often beautiful and sometimes wild and remote. Runs may also take place in local parks nearer to habitation. Wherever you compete, it will probably be on someone else's land.

We in the sport are proud of our reputation as conscientious users of sensitive countryside. We try to follow a country code. Fire is a constant threat to forested environments and can have disastrous effects on wildlife and sometimes homes. Any notices forbidding the use of matches, stoves, or cooking fires will be strictly enforced and may result in prosecution if they are disobeyed. Guard against all risks of fire and report any you see to meet officials immediately.

One of the joys of orienteering is the quiet and solitude of the forest. Don't make unnecessary noise. Enjoy the natural sounds of the forest and allow others to do so. Water is a precious resource and streams and lakes are under increasing threat from pollution. Help keep water clean by never putting anything into it. Don't bathe or swim in areas that have not been designated for that purpose.

Although crossing points may be available on a course you may need to cross a wall or a fence that does not have a natural crossing point. If you can, use a gate (closing it after you) or a stile. If you damage a wall or fence, report this to the finish officials. Meet organizers will have an agreement with the landowner about repairs to property.

You are unlikely to come across livestock, crops, or machinery but if you do, avoid any possible damage by choosing a route that avoids them. If you are confronted by a field full of crops, don't be tempted to cross it. Retrace your steps and find another route.

 **EARTHWATCH** Don't litter! When you can't find a trashcan, carry your trash with you until you find a place to put it.

5

THE BEST PLACES TO ORIENTEER

I stood on the start line, map in one hand and compass in the other. Five other competitors stood on that line, all lost in their own thoughts. Filling the air was the general buzz of conversation between officials and competitors waiting to be called to the start.

I was nervous but excited. I had been training for 6 months and this was the venue for the World Orienteering Championships in Sweden. Although I was not representing my country in the event, I was able to run the day after, over the same course, in the same forest.

The start line was at the edge of a vast, undulating forest that looked forbidding. My initial examination of the map indicated complex terrain and the promise of a great challenge. I was certain that I would need to make fast decisions about my routes through the forest. I felt as fit as I could expect for someone my age and physique, and I was a confident and experienced navigator, but this run would be the ultimate test, and I was unsure of my mental readiness.

I glanced across at my competitors on the line and drew a nervous smile from the much younger man in the next lane. This reassured me. He was younger and fitter, but he was thinking the same thoughts as I was.

The minute we all stood on the start line seemed to last forever. I had located my start position on the map and the location of the first control. I had worked out what I hoped to be a safe and reasonably quick route, and now I just wanted to start running. The wait was a good opportunity to re-examine the route, but I couldn't focus on this task. I needed to feel the ground under my feet as I ran. I needed to recognize the terrain and relate it to the map as I made my way to that first vital control.

Suddenly the buzzer sounded. Everyone on the line moved slightly forward, checked themselves, glanced again at their maps . . . and then we were off into the unknown forest.

This is my memory of my first visit to a world championship event. It was a great challenge and a wonderful opportunity to be able to run over the same terrain, using the same maps as the best in the world. One of the great joys of orienteering is its democracy. There is as yet no need to qualify for national championships—the forest has room for everyone, whatever their level of skill or expertise.

© O.N. America/Larry Berman

Orienteer Vroni Körnig of Switzerland, running in the Classic Distance Championship at the 1993 World Championships held in Harriman State Park in the Hudson Valley of New York.

Branching Out Into New Territories

Now that you have grasped the fundamentals of the sport, you need opportunities to refine your techniques. You can take full advantage of the great variety of meets, different levels of competition, and multiday festivals that are features of the orienteering scene. Competition may eventually involve considerable travel, but this in itself can be rewarding and enjoyable.

Although I have orienteered in many countries, some of my favorite experiences have been close to my home. Small club training sessions held in early summer and fall attracting no more that 50 competitors have provided me with numerous opportunities to enjoy the solitude and sounds of the forest and the splendor of color in the trees. Making a difficult route choice and hitting the control site without error can be as thrilling at a local training meet as it is at an exotic location or a multiday festival. And sometimes even in the middle of a race, unexpected beauty can give you pause. I remember once standing on a hill overlooking a huge lake dotted with islands and watching against a backdrop of snowtopped mountains an osprey fishing for its dinner. I must have looked up from my compass and map for a full 2 or 3 minutes, savoring the moment. The race, my time, and the subsequent loss of concentration hardly mattered for a short while.

WATCHING WILDLIFE

While orienteering, expect to come across a variety of birds, small mammals, deer, and maybe even some exotic creatures like my osprey when you enter their domain, the forest. The experience can be magical, but do make sure that you keep quiet and as still as possible. Don't ever approach a nest or an animal with young. If parents or their young are distressed by your presence, move quickly away.

I keep an orienteering diary and, after each meet, I make a note of my animal and bird sightings during the run. My list of sightings now includes hares, ptarmigan, deer, and foxes. Watching for animals must slow my orienteering down some, but it seems a small price to pay.

Planning for Success

Good orienteering takes good planning. When planning your orienteering year, whether it is only for yourself or for your whole family, examine all of the possibilities open to you. Joining an orienteering club is a tremendous benefit that opens many doors in the sport and should be a consideration as soon as you know this sport is for you. Most clubs are a hive of activity. Club members plan and travel together to meets and even to multiday festivals abroad.

The best planning takes advantage of whatever local meets are available and involves building up to a large meet, maybe a championship. Most club orienteers compete once a week, usually on a Saturday or Sunday, with the occasional midweek evening meet. Consider planning your competitions to begin with a number of small training sessions near home or requiring minimal travel. To improve your navigation techniques and physical fitness, each competition you enter should be in more demanding terrain than the previous one. It won't be long before you think you're familiar with all of your locally mapped areas, but this will not spoil the fun of competing there, as good course planners revisiting a forest use different areas and different control sites and legs each time. If you're running a new course, you may fail to even recognize what you thought was a familiar forest. I still make small errors in a large country park within walking distance of my home!

If you're planning to travel to a major meet or festival, think hard about its location and the time of the year it takes place. Climatic conditions can enhance or mar your experience. I recently competed in a small July meet run by Gold Country Orienteers in the Lake Tahoe area. California was baking hot at the time with record-breaking temperatures enticing many people to the beaches. High up in Tahoe, although the sun was splitting the sky, the cool mountain air and snowcapped peaks provided perfect running conditions. I combined the meet with a parasail over the lake and was able to look down from 70 meters at the forest I had run in earlier.

Trip timing is important, as anyone who has orienteered in the magnificent woodlands in New England during the fall can testify. If you plan to visit this area to compete, go in the fall to see mature woodland at its finest.

Of course, planning for a family trip will be more complex than planning only for yourself. For example, your trip goals may not coincide with those of your children. In such cases, it is probably best to plan around their likes and dislikes and make the best of the situation. Youngsters thrive on being part of the planning and decision-making process, and it helps them develop into thoughtful and responsible citizens. They like adventure and travel (as long as it is not too far and they have plenty to keep them occupied), but above all they like to be with their friends. My children grew up in an orienteering family and developed firm friendships with others in the orienteering club or with their fellow competitors in other clubs. As a parent, I was delighted to know who their friends were and what my children were doing.

At most meets your children will be with you only while traveling to the event, getting ready to compete, and during meals. The rest of the time they will be competing or playing with their friends who have also competed.

When you're taking a trip with your family, it pays to plan an orienteering day that allows time for travel to and from the meet, competition, and lunch. Leave enough time to stop at a regional area of interest on the way home.

Orienteering Vacations

Enthusiastic orienteers are increasingly following their sport on vacation. Many countries offer multiday events with 5, 6, or more days of international competition. These events attract sports tourists who wish to orienteer in new, unfamiliar terrain and link their competition to a vacation in the country. Event organizers plan sightseeing and various cultural activities for the competitors. They will normally also provide camping or trailer accommodations.

Multiday events range from the massive "O-Ringen" in Sweden, a long-established annual event, to the "Colorado 5+ Day," a new multiday event in the USA. Few orienteers have not heard of the O-Ringen, which is probably the world's premier orienteering festival. The event holds a magical attraction for orienteers, and most aspire to participate in it at least once during their life. Many orienteers compete in the O-Ringen each summer, building their vacation around the festival. The 5-day event has a paid full-time team of organizers and mappers and can attract 25,000 competitors who will compete in a different forest each day for 5 days. An event of this size requires a massive event center, lots of camping and trailer space, and the services of a small town. Competitors generally leave their vehicles parked and travel on the free buses that leave the event center at 10-minute intervals from 6 A.M. on.

The features of each O-Ringen competiton are a spectacular finish area, a swift and accurate results service, and the legendary showers. The mass showers must be seen to be believed. Each day within 300 meters of the finish line an area about 100 meters by 30 meters is screened off and divided between the sexes. Showers may have up to 100 heads, and the surrounding area resembles a green beach, with hundreds of people in various states of undress chatting, eating, or even sleeping.

© Katrin Landfors

The O-Ringen in Sweden draws thousands of competitors.

The forests chosen for this event are excellent, and the maps of the highest quality. It is surprising how a large forest swallows up so many competitors, but it does—in fact, it's possible that you'll be mainly alone as you tackle your course. A special feature of the terrain, which is seldom hilly, are the large marshes that are accurately mapped and can be used as handrails.

Established traditions of the O-Ringen are the running and development clinics. The running clinic is intended for young orienteers who eventually hope to join their international squad. Each day is devoted to improving the young orienteers' technique, and youngsters have the opportunity to be shadowed (followed) by an elite orienteer as they run through the forest. The development clinic is directed at coaches and leaders and covers such things as club development, mapping, and orienteering for the young or for people with disabilities. This is an excellent way to promote the sport worldwide, and the clinics are quite well attended.

At the other end of the multiday event scale is the Colorado 5+ Day. Don Walker, an orienteer from Boulder, promotes this popular Colorado event:

If you're looking for relaxed, friendly orienteering in beautiful runable mountain scenery (no undergrowth), glorious sunny weather, and no bugs, why not try the American Southwest? The Colorado 5+ Day, held in the last week of June each year, guarantees at least five days of orienteering, plus extras. Whether you're just getting started in orienteering or have been at it for years, you've got to try this event.

Numbers at the "5+ Day" are small enough (300 to 350) for everyone to get to know each other. Much of the special atmosphere comes from the many competitors who camp out, lending the event a sense of friendly camaraderie. Orienteers are assured a warm welcome by the local community (in 1995 the base was Lake George, a small community 50 kilometers from Colorado Springs). Already, the event is developing its own traditions. Last year, orienteers set a new record at the pancake eat-off at a local restaurant in Lake George. For the more culturally minded, the area is famous for its fossil beds, and further afield in Colorado are attractions like the world heritage site of Mesa Verde, whitewater rafting on the Colorado River, and the Rocky Mountain National Park.

Most advanced orienteering countries have recognized the popularity of multiday festivals and, with support from local and national tourist boards, devote considerable resources and time to providing a first-class orienteering experience. Multiday events bring much needed revenue to the local associations and clubs, and they generally feature new, top-quality maps that are used for local and national competitions after the event is over.

The same range of courses found at nationally sanctioned meets are available at multiday events, but, as the competitors are likely to run each day, courses are normally a little shorter.

One good reason to try a multiday event is the intensity involved in competing every day in good terrain with excellent maps and keen competition enhances your techniques. Multiday events also offer opportunities to sample different cultures, languages, and food.

The growth of orienteering throughout the world provides unlimited opportunities to visit what are often the most attractive parts of a country. In any 3-month summer period, dozens of multiday events attract substantial numbers of competitors from many different countries. Orienteering vacations are becoming so popular that an "Electronic Event Calendar" combining national fixture lists from around the world has been produced. Twenty-five federations have agreed to participate, and over 1,300 events worldwide were included for 1995. All events in the calendar include an

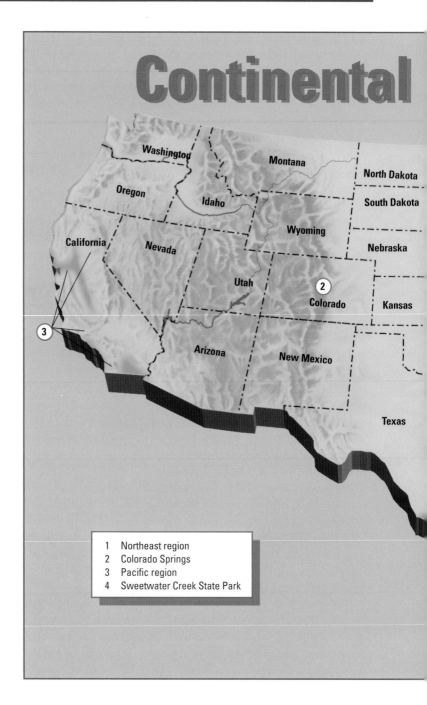

Continental

Washington
Oregon
Idaho
Montana
North Dakota
South Dakota
Wyoming
Nebraska
California
Nevada
Utah
Colorado
Kansas
Arizona
New Mexico
Texas

1   Northeast region
2   Colorado Springs
3   Pacific region
4   Sweetwater Creek State Park

United States

inquiry address. For more information, contact one of the orienteering federations listed in th appendix.

Orienteering in North America

Although North America has hosted the world championships, orienteering enthusiasts on this continent are the first to admit that the United States and Canada remain behind the top European countries, especially when it comes to the elite end of the sport. This is not because good terrain is lacking in North America, but there are far fewer competitors and media coverage of the sport is poor.

More than one top European orienteer has told me that if the United States ever sees a rapid development in orienteering, the potential exists for them to become a leading nation in the sport. Few continents have the variety and amount of wooded terrain that exists in North America. And few cultures have a population that combines relative affluence with an enthusiasm for sports.

Orienteering in the United States is thought to have begun in 1946, when Björn Kjellstrom, a champion orienteer and skier from Sweden, promoted map making and holding meets. The first meet was held in Dunes Park by Lake Michigan and was set up for Boy Scouts.

The first public meet in the states was held in the Valley Forge National Park, northwest of Philadelphia, and this led to the foundation of the oldest club in the country, Delaware Valley. The sport has spread slowly through the 1980s and 90s and, at present, 65 clubs located in most states organize events for about 10,000 regular competitors.

The United States' orienteering schedule of events is organized across eight regions that cover the continent from the northeast region, which includes New England, New York, and northern New Jersey, to the Pacific region, which covers California, Arizona, Nevada, Utah, and Hawaii.

Each club in the United States reports active mapping of new areas, the ability to host local and national meets, and terrain worthy of a visit. The success of orienteering festivals and multi-events over the past few years, along with the great distances between orienteering centers of population, should ensure that the sport continues to expand in the United States during the years ahead.

In Canada, orienteering is popular in Toronto, and festivals have been held in British Columbia, Alberta, and the Great Lakes area. Ontario's moraine terrain enables course setters (officials who design the courses and set out the controls) to provide the mental and physical challenges that are such a special feature of the sport.

The Yukon Territory has beautiful terrain for orienteering.

The Yukon Orienteering Association has hosted provincial champion-ships for the past 5 years, each on a new five-color map. The 16th Western Canadian Championships were held in 1994, north of the 60° latitude, in stunning terrain near the Yukon River. The area, a park reserve, is one of the premier outdoor recreation destinations in Canada, boasting miles of hiking, mountain biking, and ski trails. It is ideal for orienteering, with areas of complex glacial terrain in an open forest of lodge pole pine, interspersed with natural meadows and clearings. A special feature is the number of kettle hole lakes and cliffs.

As the number of clubs in the United States and Canada grows and the number of meets each year across the continent increases, standards will rise and opportunities will present themselves. In 1994, the USOF set up a working group to draw up plans for publicizing the sport and encouraging its growth in schools. This will pay off before long.

A major advantage of orienteering is the go-anywhere nature of the activity. No matter where you live in the city or in the country, you'll find small areas of woodland or parks that are being mapped by active clubs. You

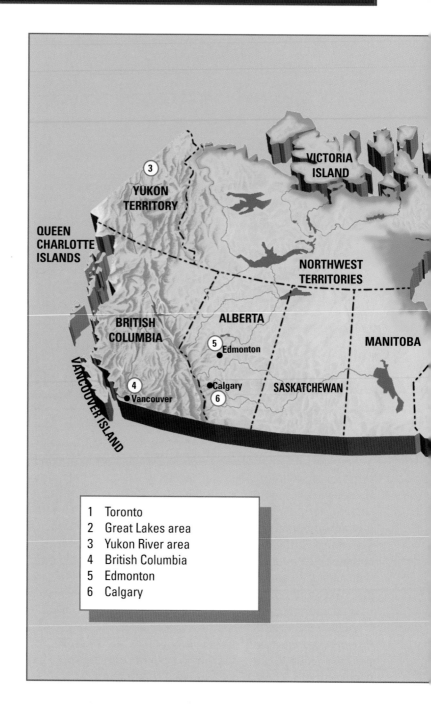

VICTORIA ISLAND

3

YUKON TERRITORY

QUEEN CHARLOTTE ISLANDS

NORTHWEST TERRITORIES

BRITISH COLUMBIA

ALBERTA

MANITOBA

5 Edmonton

VANCOUVER ISLAND

4 Vancouver

Calgary

6

SASKATCHEWAN

1 Toronto
2 Great Lakes area
3 Yukon River area
4 British Columbia
5 Edmonton
6 Calgary

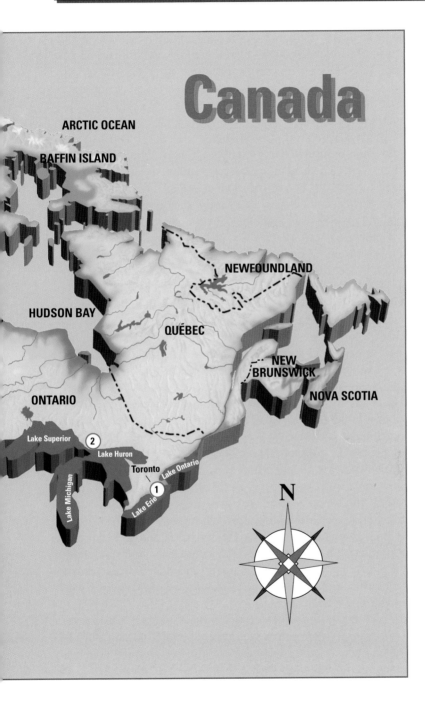

don't need large areas of woodland to practice techniques or to hold club training sessions. Color-coded courses can be held in small forests, and the courses planned to cross over and reuse a section of forest. Enterprising clubs in smaller European countries have mapped and used almost every wooded area in their vicinity. In the United States this process is just beginning, and many potential areas remain unmapped.

Because of the great distances between orienteering centers in the United States, opportunities are limited for orienteers across the continent to meet and discuss their sport. The USOF annual convention, an event unique to America, may be the answer. The convention includes 4 days of workshops, clinics, working parties, and discussion groups—in addition, of course, to the orienteering competitions. In 1994 the convention was held in Toronto, a hot bed of orienteering activity, and was linked to a 6-day festival. The Hamilton Kings Foresters of Canada celebrated its 25th anniversary as an orienteering club by organizing the event in conjunction with other clubs from Canada and the United States. The forests chosen were 100 kilometers north of Toronto and 200 kilometers northeast of Niagara Falls. Moraines from the last ice age have been sculpted into rolling hills, steep slopes, and valleys, making the terrain a challenge for orienteers. Reclaimed farmland covered by mature stands of hard wood and coniferous forest were mapped for the event. Most areas are relatively free from the thick undergrowth often associated with Canadian forests.

Canada has a larger proportion of its landmass forested than most developed countries, and orienteering is not restricted to the Toronto area. Rapid development is taking place in Western Canada. Vast travel distances have encouraged clubs to work together to develop a 3-day event in one area followed by travel time and then a 5-day event in another area.

In 1995, the "Canada 95 Orienteering Festival" began in British Columbia in high hills with some forests and sage terrain. Competitors then traveled through the Rocky Mountains and the Edmonton area to enjoy fast running on sandhill glacial moraines, pine forests, paths, and deer trails. The festival was completed in the Rocky Mountain foothills west of Calgary. The event wound up with a western banquet and dance. This form of orienteering experience makes sense in a country where travel between centers of population is extensive.

Another area of outstanding orienteering terrain is roughly 50 kilometers west of Colorado Springs (hence the development of the Colorado multiday event). For several years, local orienteering clubs in Colorado have been extensively mapping terrain at about 8,000 to 9,000 feet above sea level. They recognized the potential of one of the most extraordinary areas for orienteering in the country. Mikell Platt, a United States team member in the 1993 world championships speaks glowingly of the forests in this part of the United States.

They are coniferous and extremely open—almost park-like—with superb runability and visibility. There is no undervegetation and, while there are often many huge boulders, stony ground affecting runability is not a problem.

Mikell points out the advantage of midsummer running in Colorado:

The conditions are perfect; every day begins with cloudless blue skies, temperatures build up until it is pleasant but never too hot. Clouds begin gathering in the late afternoon, sometimes accompanied by a brief shower. By early evening, the clouds have dispersed and the stars are out in the night skies.

The multiday events in Colorado offer orienteering over granite terrain, spur/gully terrain, gneiss/schist terrain, and in areas once heavily prospected and mined. Add to this one of the most scenic tourist destinations in the United States, boasting great hiking, climbing, fishing, cycling, whitewater rafting, and numerous national parks, and you can see why this region will develop into a hot spot for orienteers.

An overview of the orienteering scene in the United States would be incomplete without mentioning the Pacific region. Bruce Wolfe, another excellent competitor now making a big contribution to the sport (including acting as the region's club development officer), reports continuous inquiries regarding club development. Areas that will be developed include Utah, Central California, and Hawaii. A new club, Gold Country Orienteers, based in Sacramento has already made inroads into local schools and is holding monthly events. An orienteering toehold in this area may spearhead growth in the direction of Yosemite and other southern Sierra areas—an exciting prospect. The San Francisco Bay area club hosts two events a month and frequent midweek training events; this has helped club membership grow to 800. The Los Angeles Orienteering Club has recently completed a number of new maps to add to its extensive collection. Their mix of 1- and 2-day events is being matched by great rivals, the San Diego Orienteers, a club in its 26th year, using nearby mountain terrain to attract orienteers throughout the region.

The benign climate of the California coast offers opportunities for year-round orienteering, and the large mobile population ensures that this part of the United States will always offer competition to residents and visitors. Orienteering in the warm summer months is at its most pleasant in the Northeast, Middle Atlantic, Northwest, and parts of the Pacific region.

In cold winter months, the warm south holds many attractions for those suffering up north. Dan Davis from the Quantico Orienteering Club in

Virginia described his visit to Sweetwater Creek State Park in Georgia as "the weekend I laid down my snow shovel and picked up my compass." Dan recounted his journey from areas buried in snow and ice to 2 days of delight in warm sunshine, with physical exercise on a competent map, friendly hosts, good food, and a great T-shirt—all at a reasonable cost. His advice is to beat the winter doldrums by heading southeast during the winter.

Orienteering in Europe

The advanced countries in Europe have a well-developed competitive structure. The Scandinavian countries, Sweden, Norway, Finland, and Denmark, are considered to have the greatest depth in terms of clubs, prime orienteering areas, maps, and numbers of competitors. In Sweden the sport is high profile, receiving much media coverage. When I attended the world championships in Skaraburg, a province in the heart of Sweden, I was one of 40,000 spectators. The organizers held open competitions for the spectators before and between the main championship race. The King of Sweden, Carl Gustav, who twice completed a cross-country ski event, went into the forest and watched competitors from a hidden position. At the end of the competition, he presented the trophies.

Scandinavia has a high proportion of forested land, and its forests are looked on as recreational assets that may be used by members of the public at will. This contrasts a common approach in other countries, where land is regarded as private and access is severely limited.

Most competitive orienteers have as a personal goal a trip to Scandinavia to take part in a multiday event. Such a trip would certainly be an opportunity to see how large-scale events can be run with super-efficiency. The orienteering season in Northern Europe is mainly in the spring, summer, and fall months, when the ground is free of snow and ice. Competing in an event in July near the Arctic Circle, when it is still light enough to map read at 11 at night, is a wonderful experience.

Although major developments have taken place in Scandinavia, where the sport originated, the sport has spread right across the continent. East Europeans from the Czech and Slovak Republics, Hungary, Poland, and the former Soviet Union have long traditions in the sport. Forests are gradually being mapped for competition, and the clubs there have the technical expertise to put on world-class and multiday events. So far, at the elite level of competition, they have not broken the stranglehold that the Swedes and Norwegians have in major competitions, but it is expected that a breakthrough will occur before too long.

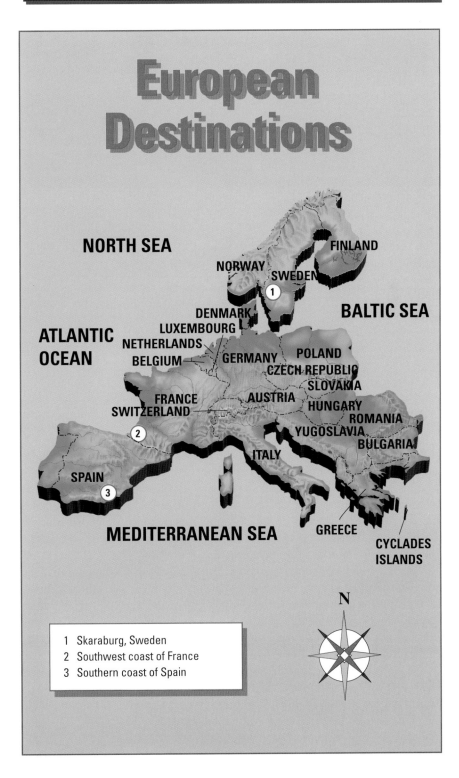

European Destinations

NORTH SEA

FINLAND

NORWAY
SWEDEN
1

BALTIC SEA

DENMARK
LUXEMBOURG

ATLANTIC
OCEAN

NETHERLANDS
BELGIUM

GERMANY
POLAND
CZECH REPUBLIC
SLOVAKIA

FRANCE
SWITZERLAND

AUSTRIA
HUNGARY
ROMANIA
YUGOSLAVIA
BULGARIA

2

SPAIN

ITALY

3

MEDITERRANEAN SEA

GREECE
CYCLADES
ISLANDS

N

1 Skaraburg, Sweden
2 Southwest coast of France
3 Southern coast of Spain

Courtesy of Orienteering World

Orienteering is becoming popular in Spain.

Orienteering in the warmer Southern European countries, France, Italy, and Spain, is also developing fast. The expanse of forested dunes in Southwest France are prime orienteering terrain that would make an excellent destination for a vacation. The terrain in these southern countries varies, but the guarantee of sunny weather and well-developed tourism enables the federations in these countries to attract people from all over the world to their summer multiday festivals.

The development occurring in Spain is typical of what's happening in the rest of the world. In 1908, a Swedish fencing instructor introduced orienteering as training for his students using a black-and-white 1:10,000 scale, hand-drawn map. In 1972, some visiting Swedes produced the first colored map, and later a series of orienteering courses was run by the orienteering "missionary" Per-Olof Bengtsson. The first Spanish club was formed in 1979. At present, over 50 clubs exist, many schools have their own map, and over 100 events at regional and local levels are staged each year. The southern coast of Spain, with its mild climate, is popular for orienteering competition and training in the midwinter months.

Orienteering in the United Kingdom

Although orienteering was not introduced here until 1962, the sport is now thriving in the UK. Domestic competition is plentiful, taking place year-round and reaching a high standard. Britain's elite orienteers are pressing for medals at the world championships, and Scotland, having recently hosted the Veteran World Championships, will host its second World Orienteering Championships in 1999.

The Scottish 6-Day Orienteering Event is a model of sports development. Every 2 years a different area of the country hosts a multiday event on new terrain. Attracting 3,000 to 4,000 competitors, these events boost local tourism and leave behind six new maps of prime orienteering terrain.

© CompassSport/Ned Paul

Most runable forrests in the UK are mapped for orienteering.

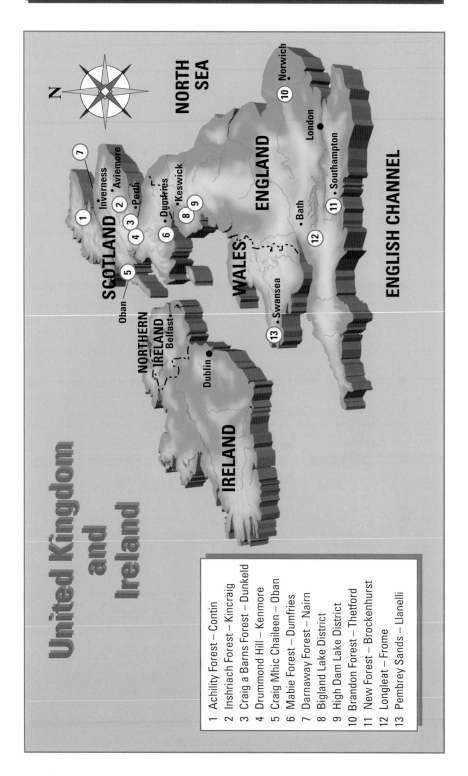

United Kingdom and Ireland

NORTH SEA

ENGLISH CHANNEL

N

SCOTLAND

ENGLAND

WALES

NORTHERN IRELAND

IRELAND

Inverness
Aviemore
Perth
Dunkires
Keswick
Oban
Belfast
Dublin
Swansea
Bath
London
Southampton
Norwich

1 Achility Forest – Contin
2 Inshriach Forest – Kincraig
3 Craig a Barns Forest – Dunkeld
4 Drummond Hill – Kenmore
5 Craig Mhic Chaileen – Oban
6 Mabie Forest – Dumfries
7 Darnaway Forest – Nairn
8 Bigland Lake District
9 High Dam Lake District
10 Brandon Forest – Thetford
11 New Forest – Brockenhurst
12 Longleat – Frome
13 Pembrey Sands – Llanelli

Scottish clubs combine resources to stage the individual days and receive a share of the profits. As a result, clubs and orienteering activity have emerged in every part of the country, and officials have acquired a technical expertise that enables them to organize major international events, such as the world championships.

Almost every forest in the United Kingdom that is accessible and runable is mapped, so there's no shortage of locations for practice and competition. In general, the terrain of highest quality is found mostly in Scotland.

Competing in Scotland is an opportunity to see a distinctive culture, magnificent scenery, and world-class organization. Other prime locations for the sport in Britain can be found in northwest England in the beautiful Lake District. You'll see my favorite forests, which are all of championship quality, plotted on the map on page 92.

Orienteers from the United States, Australia, and New Zealand often combine events in Great Britain with a short trip across the English Channel to a multiday event. This requires careful planning and can be an expensive trip, but the number of return competitors suggests that the experience is worthwhile.

Orienteering in Australia and New Zealand

As can be expected in sports-loving countries like Australia and New Zealand, orienteering is well developed though not yet a major sport. Australia hosted the 1985 world championships and the 1992 veterans championships. Likely, they will host the world championships again in 2001, a very special year for Australia, marking their centenary of federation. The plan is for the world championships events center to be in Canberra, the national capital. The competitions and training will spread between orienteering areas in the Australian capital territory and nearby parts of New South Wales.

The main objective of World Orienteering Championships 2001 is to showcase orienteering in Australia. The centenary of federation provides ideal timing, and Sydney's successful bid for the 2000 Olympics will provide media opportunities, which up to now have been limited to Scandinavia. Australia, successful in including orienteering as one of the 30 sports in the World Masters Games held in Brisbane in 1994, could be instrumental in promoting orienteering as an Olympic sport.

The Australian Orienteering Federation's blueprint shows a determination to improve schools' orienteering, promotion, talent identification, coaching, and elite competition. The country has clubs and events in all parts of the continent. Vast travel distances between states and centers of population make national competition difficult, but Australians have a popular orienteering league, where competitors score points based on their placings in each of eight individual events spread over the country. Each state has flourishing clubs and excellent terrain. Victoria is particularly well developed, with some of the best-mapped areas in the world near Ballarat. You can expect this country to eventually be a major force in the sport.

New Zealand is another country with a small population but a strong sporting tradition. Its topography is ideal for the development of orienteering. The country is renowned for its pleasant year-round climate and for superb and varied scenery, ranging from the near-tropical north to wild mountain ranges in South Island. There are around 1,500 orienteers in New Zealand with 21 clubs, mostly based in an urban center. There are four area associations that take a share of organizing national and international events. In 1994, in its 21st year, the New Zealand Orienteering Federation hosted the biannual Asia Pacific Orienteering Championships, incorporating a 6-day event. The organizers described the terrain as "intricate sand dunes, gully and spur open farmland, native bush and forest, plus open intricate land with limestone features." This description fits much of the country—one reason that the orienteer will treasure the memory of visiting this part of the world.

Courtesy of New Zealand Tourism Board

The stunning scenery and temperate climate in New Zealand are perfect for orienteering.

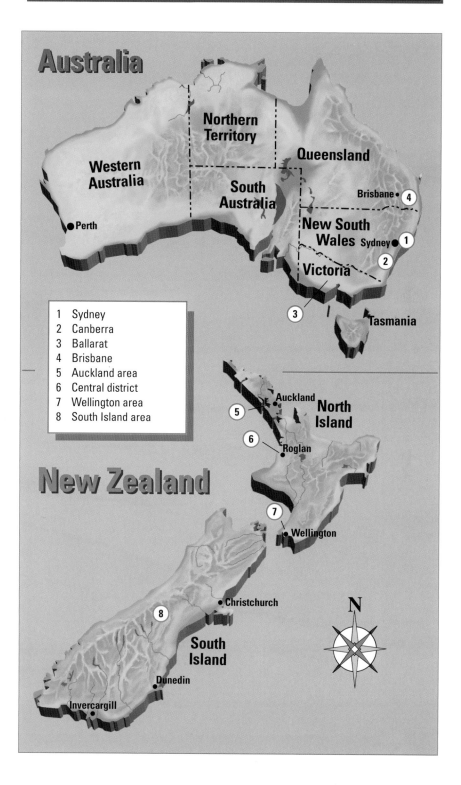

Australia

Northern
Territory

Queensland

Western
Australia

South
Australia

Brisbane ● ④

●Perth

New South
Wales Sydney ● ①

②

Victoria

③

Tasmania

1   Sydney
2   Canberra
3   Ballarat
4   Brisbane
5   Auckland area
6   Central district
7   Wellington area
8   South Island area

New Zealand

Auckland North
⑤   Island

⑥
●Roglan

⑦
●Wellington

●Christchurch

N

⑧

South
Island

●Dunedin

●Invercargill

6

PURSUING ORIENTEERING FURTHER

You have now mastered the basic techniques of orienteering. You are training and competing regularly. Are you ready to challenge yourself further and build the complex skills of the experienced orienteer? Are you ready to expand your orienteering abilities and seek new adventures?

Improve Your Skills

The competitive structures described in this book provide you with the opportunity to gain experience through a series of progressive steps within your age group, pitting your skill and fitness against those of others at similar stages. If you continue to train regularly, you'll continue to progress. Running in orienteering terrain two to three times a week, preferably with a map, will help considerably.

Once you are confident in your basic navigation, move from competing in short, easy color-coded courses to the more demanding age-group courses. Plan your orienteering season to include Class A meets and championships, and combine this with an orienteering vacation at a multiday event or festival. To continue to improve, analyze your performance after each race, draw in the route you took around the course. Estimate how much time you lost, and discuss your route with fellow competitors.

Advanced orienteering techniques are beyond the scope of this book. Our purpose here has been to introduce you to orienteering and encourage you to pursue the sport further. Specialized books dealing with advanced techniques are listed in the appendix.

Along with doing the regular training and competition recommended in this book, thinking through your strategies for competing will pay big dividends. Gaining fitness and the ability to run fast is important, but so is

© Lukas Jenzer

Regular training and competition are the best ways to improve your orienteering skills.

the ability to think fast, making decisions on the run. On all occasions keep in map contact so you are always aware of your precise location. If you make an error, correct it right away or it will compound and set you back considerably.

Gauge your technical progress by your competition results. It is usually small, simple points that give the best pay-off. Develop a self-discipline that allows you to approach each leg with the following 3-step sequence of thinking:

1. Select an attack point before you start running toward the control.

2. Choose a route to the attack point.

3. Consider techniques you'll use to reach the attack point.

Even when you are running well, feeling confident, and enjoying your orienteering, you'll occasionally make mistakes, especially in technically difficult areas and at the beginning of a race. If the going gets tough, slow down and *read the map*—think before you run.

A common error even experienced orienteers commit is called the "parallel error," that occurs when two or more similar features lie parallel to each other along the same line of travel, and you take one, thinking you are on the other. This sort of mistake can cost you a great deal of time. You can help prevent it by looking at the wider corridor of the map instead of focusing only on your line. Using your compass correctly also helps you to avoid parallel errors.

Progressing in the sport requires that you maintain concentration for the duration of each event. Concentration is often broken when you become tired or are distracted by other competitors. Practice ignoring everyone else in the race. Think only of the map and your own running. Successful competitors are able to plan one control ahead during a race. Try this, especially when you're running along a trail and don't need to watch your feet as much. If you find the opportunity to run on a trail early on, take this time to look closely at your entire course. Try to determine which legs might be the most demanding so that you can prepare for them before you reach them.

You can improve your orienteering skills by analyzing your performance after each competition. The form on pages 100-101 can help you look at the types of mistakes you made, identify why you made them, and analyze what areas you can work on to improve your skills for future races.

Finally, in your efforts to improve your level of performance, consider coaching a course yourself. Teaching others the basic techniques helps you to sharpen your own skills by making you think clearly about them.

ORIENTEERING RACE ANALYSIS

Name _____

Date _____   Map scale _____   My time _____   Min/km _____
Event _____   Class _____   Winner's time _____   Min/km _____
Weather _____   Distance _____   Lost minutes _____   Position _____

Control Point Numbers	1	2	3	4	5	6	7	8	9	10	11	12	13	14	15
Types of mistakes (put X in the box)															
Planning a route															
Executing route choice															
Rough compass															
Fine compass															
Rough map reading															
Fine map reading															
Map memory															
Use of contouring															
Caused by															
Undervalued the difficulty															
Took a chance															
Nervous															
Did not concentrate															
Tired															
Distracted by other runners															
Not used to map or scale															
Not used to terrain															

Control Point Numbers	1	2	3	4	5	6	7	8	9	10	11	12	13	14	15
The mistake happened when															
Leaving the control															
The middle of the leg															
From last attack point															
The mistake happened on															
Short leg															
Normal leg															
Long leg															
Type of ground when I missed															
Flat area															
Hilly area															
Normal area															

My main faults were

Volunteering

The best way to widen your orienteering activities is to join an orienteering club. Most clubs offer their members training and coaching courses, and they will almost certainly need help in staging an orienteering meet. If you help the club to organize a meet, you'll likely find yourself assisting at registration and car parking, and perhaps at the start or finish of a run. Most club orienteers can do this and manage to fit in a run for themselves as well.

Course Planning

As you gain experience, you may wish to qualify to be a course planner (setter). Setting a course can be very creative and rewarding, as it involves planning each of the courses and hanging the controls. Pitting your wits against the competitors is a challenge and will undoubtedly sharpen your map reading. Course planners must place each control in exactly the correct place on the ground, so they will inevitably obtain practice in map reading and interpreting maps correctly.

Orienteering on Permanent Courses

Putting out, and collecting in, orienteering controls for a meet is time-consuming and ensures that orienteering can take place only over a specific period of time. In many countries, orienteering clubs have worked with parks or land owners to have controls placed on a permanent basis. Permanent courses are usually near centers of population in any wooded area that has a suitable orienteering map. Posts, instead of the usual orienteering controls, are placed in the ground and a code attached to each one.

For most permanent courses, maps are available with the control sites premarked—or a master map may be provided. You can use these permanent control sites to practice your techniques or to simulate real orienteering courses. In Scandinavia this is called "trim" orienteering, but most other countries use the term "wayfinding." Your local orienteering club or federation (see the appendix) can tell you where to find the nearest permanent courses to you. Most cities in the United Kingdom have a permanent course in some of their parks. These courses are maintained and changed at intervals by local orienteering clubs who see them as a way of assisting school orienteering and attracting newcomers to the sport.

Orienteering courses with permanent control sites are good places to practice technique.

Street Orienteering

In some countries the climate prevents orienteering in the forest during summer, when there is a risk of forest fire. In these months, enterprising clubs put on evening events using town centers and the street network. The maps they use are usually foolscap size (21x30 cm) and based on the local street guide. (Black-and-white photocopies are cheaper but perfectly adequate for this form of competition.) Control markers may be improvised in the form of metal plates or cord fastened to features such as "telegraph pole," "fence end," or "picnic table." These street events are popular with club members as they prevent fitness loss during the off-season. Street orienteering promotes map reading on the run, preplanning, and leaving the control site quickly. This kind of orienteering is not normally recorded in the fixture lists published by federations but may be noted in club newsletters or magazines.

Night Orienteering

Dark winter evenings may be used to introduce night orienteering. Courses are usually available for people over 15 years old and are held in open or semi-open areas where the darkness reduces visibility. Competitors use powerful head torches (with rechargeable batteries). The head torch is strapped to the forehead and the batteries are attached to the upper body. This arrangement reduces the amount of weight carried on the forehead and prevents the light moving about.

Night orienteering helps you develop the ability to make map contact immediately and maintain it. You use the compass carefully and make use of trails to make progress. Don't try this form of the sport until you have grasped the basic techniques of orienteering and have confidence in your ability. You might try running courses with a friend until you're comfortable in the darker environment. Once you've learned the basics, night orienteering is fun.

Sprint Orienteering

Sprint orienteering is gaining popularity each year, and most federations report increasing numbers of competitions. Sprint orienteering courses are shorter than the traditional courses and competitors attempt to run the entire course at top speed. Start times ensure that other competitors are running directly against you as they would on a track. This kind of orienteering demands quick decision making and the ability to recover quickly from errors. It can be an exciting event to watch, as competitors sometimes cross the finish line within seconds of each other. The key to sprint orienteering is the ability to trade off speed against accuracy. Try sprint orienteering as a way to increase your running speed and sharpen your techniques. Don't compare your speed to that of other competitors—instead find the fastest speed your lungs, legs, and map-reading skills can cope with.

Rogaining or Mountain Marathons

In a rogaine, teams of at least two travel over a large area using a map and compass to find controls that gain points. They try to amass the highest total within a time limit, which may be as long as 24 hours. This form of orienteering is clearly for the ultrafit who enjoy the challenge of long-distance running in hilly and often remote countryside. In the United

Rogaining is for highly skilled and fit orienteers.

Kingdom, an annual event, the Karrimor Mountain Marathon, attracts up to 4,000 competitors. Six courses are offered varying from 40K to 70K in distance. In the "KIMM" one of the courses is similar to the American rogaine and known as a "score event." Competitors select their own route to gain as many points as possible within a time limit of 5 or 6 hours over 2 days. The other courses are similar to normal orienteering courses except for the greater distances involved. All competitors camp overnight and subsequently have to carry their tent and food in a rucksack.

Ski Orienteering

Although orienteering has been recognized as an Olympic sport by the International Olympic Committee, it has not yet found its way into Olympic competition. When it does it will probably be ski orienteering that is accepted as a demonstrator sport.

Ski orienteering events comprise long distance, short distance, and relay. Planned winning times are similar to those of foot orienteering. In long-distance ski orienteering the distances between controls are greater and the trail network less dense. The competitors need to take altitude into account

THE LIFE OF A NOMAD

A competitor in the "Swiss KIMM" describes the fascination of this form of competition:

I gradually get used to orienteering in the high mountains and to running with a rucksack on my back. The spirit of this adventurous orienteering competition gains the upper hand. Up and up we go until we finally reach the fourth control right on the Swiss-Austrian border and, at 2,683 meters, today's highest point. Then down into the valley, over scree slopes and snowfields. A young Australian, who has flashed past me on some scree, immediately becomes slow and uncertain in the snow. Not surprising, really—how could an Aussie have experienced snow before? After 6 hours, Fritz and I reach the midway camp, situated at 2,100 meters in a corrie. As incoming teams put up more and more small tents, a little "orienteering town" forms. Fritz cooks our evening meal while I fetch the water. Darkness falls, and we creep into our sleeping bag. The nomadic life!

and choose the best trails. In the short-distance form of the sport there is usually a dense pattern of trails and the decisive factors are map-reading ability while skiing, and skiing the chosen trails without stopping too frequently. In relays, a combination of the two styles is appropriate.

Foot orienteering maps (without dark green) can be used for ski orienteering. If possible, trails should be flat—organizers achieve this by running a snowmobile over the trails before the competition. The trails are printed in green on the map, in a continuous line for fast trails, a broken line for good trails, and a dotted line for narrow, winding, and slow trails.

The start and finish areas in ski orienteering are normally in the same place on open ground. Most courses are planned so that skiers on two or three loops are visible to spectators. Group starts (distinct from the individual starts in foot orienteering) with forked courses add to the excitement.

In large events, radio and TV controls inform spectators at the finish area how individual competitiors are progressing, and in group starts, the first person crossing the finish line is the winner—a big attraction to the media and sponsors. Ski orienteering is most popular in the Scandinavian countries, but the sport will likely spread to all countries that participate in winter sports.

Mountain Bike Orienteering

Mountain biking has become a major outdoor pastime throughout the world. The sales of mountain bikes in Western Europe now outstrip those of all other forms of cycles. Orienteers attracted to this activity have combined it with their own sport.

Orienteering on mountain bikes (OMB) is new, but about a dozen countries report that events are being organized officially. OMB is an exciting sport that demands the same kind of physical and mental aptitude that foot or ski orienteering require. Cycling off the trails is forbidden, and the "cyclability" of trails is shown on the map in green overprinting. Technical organization is relatively simple, and as long as the environmental

© CompassSport/Rob Howard

Mountain bike orienteering combines two popular sports.

damage that mountain bikes can do is controlled, this form of orienteering will continue to grow in popularity. The first international match was held in France in 1994; the event was so successful that many are sure to follow.

Orienteering for People With Disabilities

Orienteers have increasingly been considering possible ways for people with disabilities to participate in the sport. Research is underway into types of provision for the blind or partially sighted and for others who have learning difficulties. A form of the sport, called "trail orienteering," has been devised for those with physical disabilities, including wheelchair users. "Trail-O" is rare among sports in that the physical capacity of the competitor has no bearing on the competition result. The objective is not to get around the course as quickly as possible but to visit each control in order and complete demanding navigational tasks. Points are awarded for accuracy in map reading and interpretation rather than for choosing a route and finding the control quickly.

© Richard B. Levine

The emphasis on accessibility for people with disabilities makes orienteering popular with wheelchair athletes.

In Trail-O, competitors are given a map with a course drawn on it and leave the start for the first control. They cannot, however, leave the path network. Competitors reach a point where they can see the control site area from the path. They view two, three, or four red and white markers hanging on different but often similar features and must determine which one is located at the point indicated by the center of the one control circle on their map. At most controls there is no time limit for deciding which marker is in the correct location, but at one or two controls the decision-making process is timed. The timed controls are used only in a tie-break situation, when competitors have an equal number of correctly identified controls.

This multichoice orienteering with false controls allows a number of people with different disabilities and different degrees of disability to compete on equal terms.

Although these competitors cannot experience the joy of running through the forest, they can share the delights of being in the woods and concentrating on map and terrain interpretation, activities that wheelchair users greatly appreciate. This form of the sport is sure to be adopted by countries across the world who wish as many people as possible to enjoy the exciting and fulfilling sport of orienteering.

MAKING CONNECTIONS

Jacques Eloy, who has multiple sclerosis, writes about his experience of trail orienteering after competing in the European championships:

I always loved to take to the road for a walk into nature, but I often felt frustrated after my aimless wanderings. For me, trail orienteering was an opportunity to discover new landscapes and meet other nature lovers. I had to learn map reading and terrain interpretation, which I find fascinating. At the competition I made contact with disabled competitors from Belgium, Germany, the United Kingdom, and Lithuania. Hand speaking and smiling were effective in communicating. During the competition, I took the opportunity to observe the environment, identifying among other plants an orchid named Orchis Maculata. After the race, in which I finished second, I exchanged addresses and compared the ways of life in other countries for those in similar situations to mine. I found trail orienteering to be a wonderful, enlightening adventure.

Join Me?

Twenty years ago, when I first got involved in orienteering, I didn't realize that it would lead to so many memorable occasions and play such an important part in my life. Orienteering is an exciting adventure sport that welcomes all comers to join in and share the wonders of the forest, the challenges of the course planners, and the camaraderie of fellow competitors. I know I'll be running through sunlit forests, enjoying the sights and sounds of nature and feeling the thrill of the race for as long as my legs will carry me. Come join me!

APPENDIX

FOR MORE INFORMATION

Federations

Orienteering Federation of Australia
PO Box 740
Glebe, NSW 2037
Australia
61 2 660 2067; Fax 61 2 660 6661

Österreichischer Fachverbank für OL
Prinz Eugenstr.
12 A-1040 Wien
Austria
Phone and fax 43 1 505 03 93; Tlx. 133 132

Association Belge des Sports d'Orientation
c/o J. Herremans
Meerhoef 12
B-3971 Heppen
Belgium
32 11 34 3301; Fax 32 11 34 8906

The Canadian Orienteering Federation
Suite 408, 1600 James Naismith Dr.
Gloucester, Ontario K1B 5N4
Canada
613-748-5649; Fax 613-748-5602; Tlx. 053-3660

Dansk Orienterings-Forbund
Idraettens Hus, Bröndby Stadion 20
DK-2605 Bröndby, Denmark
45 42 45 77 30; Fax 45 43 45 77 90; Tlx. 33 111

Agrupacion Espanola de Clubes de Orientacion (A.E.C.O.)
Secretario General D. Eusebio Garcia Gomez
Gran Via, 66-8-16, E-28013
Madrid, Spain
34 1 542 0880

Suomen Suunnistusliitto
Radiokatu 20
FIN-00240 Helsinki, Finland
358 0 158 2329; Fax 358 0 158 24 33; Tlx.12 1797

Fédération Francaise de Course d'Orientation
BP 220, F-75967
Paris Cedex 20, France
33 1 47 97 11 91; Fax 33 1 47 97 90 29

British Orienteering Federation, Riversdale
Dale Road North, Darley Dale
Matlock, Derbyshire DE4 2HX
England
44 1629 734 042; Fax 44 1629 733 769

Deutscher Turner Bund, Abteilung Sport
Orientierungslauf
Otto-Fleck-Schneisse 8
D-60528 Frankfurt am Main
Germany
49 69 67 80 10; Fax 49 69 67 80 11 79; Tlx. 411 5113

Irish Orienteering Association
House of Sport, Longmile Road
Walkinstown, Dublin 12
Ireland
353 1 50 98 45, 1 56 90 99; Fax 353 1 50 28 05

Federazione Italiana Sport Orientamento
Corso 3 Novembre, 36 Cas. Post. 640
I-38100 Trento
Italy
39 461 916 900; Fax 39 461 916 308

Nederlandse Orienteringsloop Bond
Secretary Jody Borgers
Klaverstraat 80, NL-3572 VG Utrecht
The Netherlands
31 30 27 21 131

Norges Orienteringsforbund,
Hauger Skolevei 1, N-1351 Rud
Norway
47 67 15 46 00; Fax 47 67 15 47 86; Tlx. 78 586

New Zealand Orienteering Federation
Secretary: Les Warren
PO Box 145
Morrinsville, New Zealand
64 7 889 7608

Federacao Portuguesa de Orientacao
Apartado 2
P-2640 Mafra, Portugal
351 61 51 524; Fax 351 61 81 2710

Schweizerischer Orientierungslauf-Verband
Marianne Bandixen
Langweidstrasse 2
CH-8620 Wetzikon
Switzerland
41 1 932 50 80; Fax 41 1 932 50 84

Svenska Orienteringsförbundet
Idrottens Hus, S-123 87 Farsta
Sweden
46 8 605 60 00; Fax 46 8 605 63 60; Tlx. 141 79

United States Orienteering Federation
PO Box 1444
Forest Park, GA 30051
USA
404-363-2110; Fax 404-363-2110

Ski Orienteering

Svenska Skidförbundet
Idrottens Hus, S-123 87 Farsta
Sweden
46 8 605 60 00; Fax 46 8 93 89 80

Dansk Skidforbund
Idraettens Hus, Bröndby Stadion 20
DK-2605 Bröndby
Denmark
45 43 26 23 31; Tlx. 33 111

Russian Ski-Orienteering Association (RSOA)
Secretary Anatoly Shigaev
Luzhnetskaja nab 8
Moscow 119270
Russia
7 095 201 1701; Fax 7 095 499 0401

United States Orienteering Federation Member Clubs by Region

Northeast

Western Connecticut OC (WCOC)
c/o Rick De Witt
390 Szost St.
Fairfield, CT 06430

New England OC (NEOC)
c/o Joanne Sankus
9 Cannon Road
Woburn, MA 01801

Cambridge Sports Union (CSU)
c/o Larry Berman
23 Fayette St.
Cambridge, MA 02139

Hudson Valley O' (HVO)
c/o Dave Hodgdon
106 Allentown Rd.
Parsippany, NJ 07054

Hudson Valley Orienteering
(HVO)
PO Box 61
Pleasantville, NY 10570

Empire OC (EMPO)
PO Box 51
Clifton Park, NY 12065

Buffalo OC (BFLO)
c/o Dave Cady
148 Humboldt Parkway
Buffalo, NY 14214

Rochester OC (ROC)
c/o Richard Detwiler
422 Woodland Lane
Webster, NY 14580

Central NY O' (CNYO)
c/o Barb Sleight
6187 Smith Rd.
N. Syracuse, NY 13212-2513

Long Island OC (LIOC)
c/o John Pekarik
238 Loop Dr.
Sayville, NY 11782

Adirondack OK (AOK)
c/o Brian McDonnell
168 Lake Flower Ave.
Saranac Lake, NY 12983

US Military Academy OC
(USMA)
c/o Dept. of Geography and
Environmental Engineering
West Point, NY 10996

Orienteering Unlimited OC (OU)
c/o Ed Hicks
3 Jan Ridge Rd.
Somers, NY 19589

Wilderness Orienteering Camps
(WOC)
PO Box 202
Mahapac, NY 10541

Green Mountain OC (GMOC)
c/o Jim Howley
41 McIntosh Ave.
S. Burlington, VT 05403

Mid-Atlantic

Delaware Valley O' Association
(DVOA)
c/o Mary Frank
14 Lake Dr.
Spring City, PA 19475

Indiana University of Penn.
(IUPOC)
c/o Jim Wolfe
319 Stright IUP
Indiana, PA 15705

Susquehanna Valley Orienteering
(SVO)
c/o Michael Ball
5587 Mercury Rd.
Harrisburg, PA 17109

Land of the Vikings (LOVOC)
Sherman PA SON Lodge
c/o Svein Sedeniussen
270 Ehrhardt Rd.
Pearl River, NY 10965

Pocono OC (POC)
PO Box 245
Pocono Lake, PA 18347-0245

Warrior Ridge OC (WROC)
c/o Michael Lubich
PO Box 191
Rice's Landing, PA 15356

Quantico OC (QOC)
6212 Thomas Dr.
Springfield, VA 22150

Fork Union Military Academy OC
(FUMA)
c/o LTC Fred Tucker
FUMA
Fork Union, VA 23055

Southeast

Vulcan OC (VOC)
c/o Graeme Wilson
196 Deer Mountain
Indian Springs, AL 35124

Florida O' (FLO)
c/o Frank Kuhn
3150-334 N. Harbor City Blvd.
Melbourne, FL 32935

Georgia OC (GADC)
c/o Bill Cheatum
1720 S. Lumpkin St.
Athens, GA 30606

Blue Star Komplex (BSK)
c/o Fred Zendt
355 Balboa Ct.
Atlanta, GA 30342

Backwoods OK (BOK)
c/o Treklite
904 Dorothea Dr.
Raleigh, NC 27603

Triad OC (TRIAD)
c/o Joe Halloran
1820 Ardsley St.
Winston-Salem, NC 27103

Carolina OK (COK)
PO Box 220362
Charlotte, NC 28222

Tennessee OC (TOC)
c/o Meg Garrett
1747 Murfreesboro Hwy.
Manchester, TN 73755

Mid-West

O' Louisville (OLOU)
PO Box 7773
Louisville, KY 40257

Southern Michigan OC (SMOC)
c/o Bill Luitje
2677 Wayside Dr.
Ann Arbor, MI 48103

North Eastern Ohio OC (NEOH)
PO Box 5703
Cleveland, OH 44101-0703

Orienteering Club of Cincinnati (OCIN)
c/o Pat Meehan
1306 Southern Hills Blvd.
Hamilton, OH 45013-3738

Miami Valley OC (MVOC)
c/o Frederick Dudding
2533 Far Hills Ave.
Dayton, OH 45419

Central Ohio O' (COO)
c/o Michael Minium
5412 College Corner Pike #113
Oxford, OH 45056

Heartland

Rocky Mountain OC (RMOC)
c/o Steve Willman
710 Sunnywood Place
Woodland Park, CO 80863

Chicago Area OC (CAOC)
PO Box 4591
Wheaton, IL 60189

Iowa OC (IOC)
c/o Carl Thurman
2130 Rainbow Dr.
Waterloo, IA 50701

Orienteer Kansas (OK)
c/o Gene Wee
2223 Westchester Rd.
Lawrence, KS 66049

Minnesota OC (MNOC)
PO Box 580030
Minneapolis, MN 55458

St. Louis OC (SLOC)
c/o Al Smith
74 Decorah Dr.
St. Louis, MO 63146

Possum Trot OC (PTOC)
c/o Alan Cowles
11512 W. 101st Terr.
Overland Park, KS 66214

N. Dakota O'Allnce (NCOA)
c/o Michelle Keller
PO Box 265
Bisbee, ND 58317

Badger OC (BGR)
c/o Catherine Ann Yekenevicz
868 Weslyn Ct. #2
West Bend, WI 53095

Southwest

ARK-LA-TEX O'SOCIETY (ALTOS)
PO Box 8792
Bossier City, LA 71113-8792

Sooner OC (SOON)
c/o Grafton Potter
4715 E. 105th Pl.
Tulsa, OK 74137

Houston OC (HOC)
c/o Carolyn Ortegon
PO Box 18251
Houston, TX 77023

North Texas O Assn. (TNOA)
PO Box 832464
Richardson, TX 75083-2464

Hill Country OC (HCOC)
c/o Steve Nelson
45 Eskew Lane
Cedar Creek, TX 78612

Aggie Pathfinders (AGGIE)
PO Box 8592
College Station, TX 77844

Pacific

Tucson OC (TSN)
PO Box 13012
Tucson, AZ 85732

Phoenix OC (PHXO)
c/o Fred Padgett
2031 N. 16th St.
Phoenix, AZ 85006

Bay Area OC (BOC)
c/o Gary Kraght
518 Park Way
Mill Valley, CA 94941

Los Angeles OC (LAOC)
c/o Clare Durand
5341 Wilkinson Ave., #3
N. Hollywood, CA 91607

San Diego Orienteering (SDO)
c/o Bill Gookin
PO Box 26722
San Diego, CA 92196

Gold Country Orienteers (GCO)
c/o Dwight Freund
2948 Leta Lane
Sacramento, CA 95821

Utah Governor's Council on
Health and Physical Fitness
Darlene Uzelac
PO Box 16660
Salt Lake City, UT 84116

Northwest

Arctic OC (ARCT)
c/o Daniel Ellsworth
6436 Carlos Ct.
Anchorage, AK 99504

Columbia River OC (CROC)
c/o Matthew Boser
1700 NE 162nd Ave. #E2
Portland, OR 97230

Jefferson State OC (JSOC)
c/o Allyson Kelley
PO Box 1371
Medford, OR 97301

Cascade OC (COC)
PO Box 31375
Seattle, WA 98103

Chuckanut Orienteers (CHUKO)
c/o Ken and Joanne Klepsch
4313 Tyler Way
Anacortes, WA 98221

Eastern Washington OC (EWOC)
PO Box 944
Spokane, WA 99210

Ellensburg OC (EOC)
c/o Willard Sperry
1006 N. Water St.
Ellensburg, WA 98926

Husky OC (HUSKY)
c/o Eric Bone
HUB 207 FK-30
Box 118
Univ. of Washington
Seattle, WA 98195

Nisqually O' (NISQ)
c/o Carl Moore
1453 N. Winnifred
Tacoma, WA 98406

Sacajawea Orienteers (SACO)
c/o Elis Eberstein
520 Meadows Dr. S.
Richland, WA 99352

Sammamish OC (SAMM)
PO Box 3682
Bellevue, WA 98009

Books

Pathways to Excellence
P Palmer, Harvey's
12-16 Main St.
Doune, Perthshire FK16 6BJ
Scotland (£9.95)

Skills of the Game—Orienteering
C McNeill, Crowood Press
Ramsbury, Marlborough
Wiltshire SN8 2HE
England (£8.95)

Start Orienteering (a series of five books)
C McNeill and T Renfrew, Harvey's
12-16 Main St.
Doune, Perthshire FK16 6BJ
Scotland (£4.95 per book)

Teaching Orienteering
C McNeill, J Ramsden, and T Renfrew; Harvey's
12-16 Main St.
Doune, Perthshire FK16 6BJ
Scotland (£19.95)

Trail Orienteering
A. Braggins, Harvey's 12-16 Main St.
Doune, Perthshire FK16 6BJ
Scotland (£9.95)

Magazines/Journals

Compass Sport: The Orienteer
25 The Hermitage, Eliot Hill
London, S.E.13 7EH
United Kingdom
0181 552 1457

Orienteering World
International Orienteering Federation
Box 76
S-191 21 Sollentuna
Sweden
46 835 3455; Fax 46 835 7168

Orienteering North America
SM & L. Berman Publishing Co.
23 Fayette Street
Cambridge, MA 02139 USA
1-617-868-7416

The Australian Orienteer
PO Box 263
Jamison Centre, ACT 2614
Australia
61 6 251 3885

New Zealand Orienteering
c/o Bruce Collins
Ontonga Valley Road
RD1 Raglan
New Zealand
64 7 825 5745

ORIENTEERING LINGO

aiming off—A technique involving deliberately aiming to one side of a point on a linear feature so there is only one way to turn to find a control.

attack point—A large feature close to the control used in selecting and executing a route.

base plate—The part of the compass that holds the compass housing.

bearing—The direction you want to travel.

class—Age groups for men's and women's competition.

contact—A term used for relating map to ground or ground to map.

control—The marker on the control site identified on the map by a circle.

control card—Card orienteers carry to mark each control they visit.

control code—Identification letters or numbers displayed at the control site and included on the description list.

collecting feature—A long feature used as a point of reference during the route or to keep you from running too far beyond a control.

course—The start, controls, and finish that all orienteers pass through.

course planner—The designer of the courses in a competition. Also called the course setter.

dog leg—A poorly planned leg that allows orienteers entering the control area to see others ahead leaving that area and thus gaining advantage.

event—An organized competition. Also called a meet.

Fartlek—A Swedish word meaning "speed play." An undisciplined interval session where you run quickly, recover, run quickly again, and so on. The recovery phase is a slow jog.

fight—Impenetrable forest shown on the map as dark green.

fine orienteering—Precise navigation, keeping map contact throughout.

form-line—An intermediate contour line shown as a broken line on the map. Half the normal height higher than the contour line below.

handrail—A line feature that can be used to aid navigation and simplify map reading.

key— A list of symbols represented on the map. Also called a legend.

knoll—A small hill shown on the map by a brown dot or a small brown circle or form line.

leg—The section of the course between any two consecutive control points.

legend—A list of symbols represented on the map. Also called a key.

master map—Is used to copy courses onto orienteers' maps.

magnetic-north lines—Shown on all orienteering maps as an aid to using the compass.

meet—An organized competition. Also called an event.

orienting the map—Turning the map until north on the map points to north on the terrain. Also called setting the map.

photogrammetry—The use of air photographs to produce a base map, which is then used for surveying.

pace counting—Counting double paces to measure distance covered on the ground.

prestart—The orienteer's call-up time, usually 2 minutes before the start time.

premarked maps—Maps given at the prestart with your course printed on it.

punch—Instrument found at each control and used by an orienteer to mark the control card. Each punch has a distinctive set of needles.

ride—A linear gap in the forest often designated as a fire break.

re-entrant—A small valley.

relocation—Finding your position on the map when originally lost.

rough orienteering—Running quickly, collecting the major features along the route.

setting the map—Turning the map until north on the map points to north on the terrain. Also called orienting the map.

string course—A short course marked on the terrain by a continuous line of string.

stub—Part of the control card handed in at the prestart and used as a check by the organizers to determine who is in the forest.

thumbing—Holding the map folded in a way that your thumb can move to follow your position on the map.

INDEX

ABOUT THE AUTHOR

Tom Renfrew, an expert orienteer and a top instructor in the U.K. for more than 20 years, has developed and taught orienteering techniques and programs across the U.S. and in Europe. Since discovering the excitement of orienteering in 1976, he has been involved in the sport from the grass roots to the international level. Considered the leading authority on the educational values of the sport, Tom has been a driving force behind the development of orienteering in the national school curriculum throughout the United Kingdom.

After earning an advanced diploma in physical education from the University of Leeds in 1971 and a bachelor's degree in educational studies in 1977 from the Open University, Tom completed a master of science degree at Stirling University in 1983. His research has subsequently focused on introducing and developing orienteering techniques, adapting orienteering opportunities for people with disabilities, mainstreaming individuals with disabilities into orienteering, and teaching map skills to those with learning difficulties.

Director of sport and outdoor education at the University of Strathclyde, Tom has written eight books, including *Teaching Orienteering* and *Orienteering for Children*, and has created audiovisual resources that are used worldwide. He is a member of the British Orienteering Federation and has served as chair of its Coaching Committee.

Tom resides in Beardsden, Scotland. He shares his love of orienteering with his wife, Fiona, and their children.

Other books in the

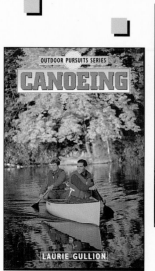

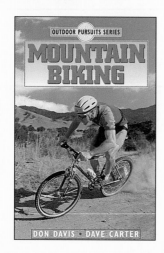

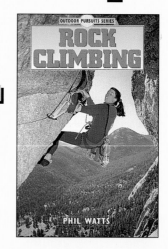

Outdoor Pursuits Series

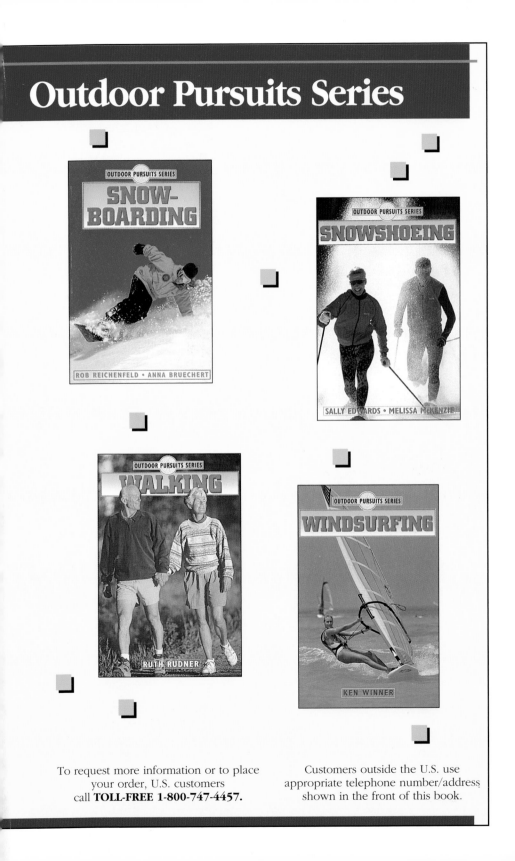

OUTDOOR PURSUITS SERIES
SNOW-BOARDING
ROB REICHENFELD • ANNA BRUECHERT

OUTDOOR PURSUITS SERIES
SNOWSHOEING
SALLY EDWARDS • MELISSA McKENZIE

OUTDOOR PURSUITS SERIES
WALKING
RUTH RUDNER

OUTDOOR PURSUITS SERIES
WINDSURFING
KEN WINNER

To request more information or to place
your order, U.S. customers
call **TOLL-FREE 1-800-747-4457.**

Customers outside the U.S. use
appropriate telephone number/address
shown in the front of this book.